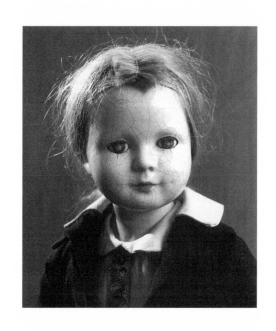

ENCHANTED COMPANIONS

For everyone who has loved a doll.

ENCHANTED COMPANIONS

Stories of Dolls in Our Lives

Carolyn Michael and Friends

Carolyn Michael

Storyweaver

Library of Congress Catalogue number 00-090586
Enchanted companions: stories of dolls in our lives / by Carolyn Michael and Friends
1. Biography 2. Memoir
ISBN 0-9679111-0-9

First Edition
Printed in Canada
Cover design: Clare Conrad
Text design: Carolyn Michael and Clare Conrad

Photo credits
Cover: courtesy of Diane Picard Fleming picturing
Dianne Hicks Morrow, Diane Picard Fleming, and Bonnie Howard Warner.
Title page, author photo and doll group (page 173) by Kari Berger.
Dedication photo by Pamela Frierson picturing her daughter, Delta.
Memoriam photo by Ferd Herres.
Page 176: Virginia Wise by Vance Orchard
Back cover photos: Carolyn Michael by Ferd Herres; Floyd Bell courtesy of Floyd Bell;
Nina Munk courtesy of Ann Teplick; Dorothy Wilcox by Carol Severance.

Storyweaver
1910 East 4th Ave. PMB #91
Olympia, WA 98506-4632

In memory of my son
Brad Burns
who loved and slept with stuffed animals all his 28 years.

Contents

Introduction

As birds make a nest of anything,
children make a doll of no matter what.

—Victor Hugo, *Les Miserables*

My son Ryan and I were munching burritos in a fast food joint one afternoon, swapping stories. Out of the corner of my eye, I noticed a woman and her two young daughters talking excitedly at a nearby table. A number was called and the mother grabbed her wallet from her purse and left to get their food. The younger girl picked up her mother's fake alligator handbag and drew circles on it with her finger. "Look," she said to her sister, "Here are the eyes, here is the nose and here is the mouth." She hugged it to her heart, closed her eyes and gently rocked it side to side.

Ryan and I looked at one another and laughed. We had just been contemplating the timeless, universal and mysterious appeal of dolls. I had shared with him some of the doll stories I had recently gathered. There was the grandmother who wanted to have her childhood doll cremated with her when she died. A man told of being confined at home with an injury when he was a boy because of lack of accessibility to medical care in his homeland of Ghana. Day after day, he watched his little sisters make dolls out of mango seeds, taking care that the fibers stayed attached to serve as hair. They enacted family scenarios and held their tiny babies to their breasts to nourish them. Ryan and I searched for ways to explain these magical bonds, but perhaps it is the mystery of a doll's powerful hold that draws us to them again and again.

My story-gathering began in 1993 when I attended a writing retreat on tranquil Saltspring Island, British Columbia, with ten other women. We wrote several hours a day and each morning our facilitator read excerpts from the previous day's writings. These personal, emotionally rich stories provoked both tears and laughter. One story, however, stayed in my mind, becoming the genesis of this book. It was Susan Berlin's story, "Who Would I Tell?" She recounted her elderly mother's sharing of bittersweet memories of a special doll, expressing strong emotions held for over eighty years. The ending of Susan's moving tale affected me so deeply that I was inspired for the next five years to collect people's memories of their dolls. I thought of all the people in the world with stories to tell and perhaps with no one to listen to them. I wanted to give people the opportunity to recall and share important moments in their lives that centered around relationships with dolls. Besides giving me the pleasure of hearing countless personal tales, it gave me the opportunity to again contemplate the mystery of our human attraction to dolls and my own lifelong love of these inanimate playmates.

I began telling everyone that I was gathering stories about dolls. The response was almost as universal as dolls themselves. First there'd be a pause, then a tentative "I have a doll story," followed by an eagerness to share an experience. Stories began coming to me from all directions, including people I met on the bus. But my friends obliged me first, writing me their stories in their own words, allowing their unique voices and experiences to come forth. Some people were comfortable writing and others were nearly terrified at the notion, so a few came to my home for small group writing sessions to help get them started. No definition of "doll" was given, just encouragement to write without stopping or editing one's thoughts.

When a completed story was given to me, I set aside a special time to read it, to savor it. Time after time, I was astonished by the profound nature of the stories. Each friend had looked deep inside and presented me with a precious gift, allowing me the freedom to share it however I chose. I continue to be filled with gratitude for the generosity of my friends, for their trust and love.

And then I asked for photos, which sent my friends scouring their family albums. A few found photos of themselves with the doll they had written about, others sent pictures of themselves at the age they were when their story took place. Some didn't have photographs, so they brought me dolls that had been tucked away. Kari Berger came with her camera equipment and creative photographer's eye, spending hours positioning the dolls, adjusting the lights, capturing different moods on seemingly static faces.

As the project began to take on a life of its own, I realized I needed to make some difficult choices. I saw how creating this book was similar to making a doll, an art I have been enjoying for several years. When I make a doll, I have an idea about how I want it to be. I gather together all sorts of wonderful fabrics, embellishments and doo-dahs, wanting to use them all. But as I shape and play and experiment, the doll begins to form herself. Sometimes I try over and over to add some favorite piece of fabric and the doll says, "No, put it aside for another time." And so it has been with some of the stories given to me. Though they are not all printed here, every story I heard or that was written for me is an integral part of the fabric and texture of this book.

"The greatest gift we can give one another is our stories," celebrated writer Isabel Allende told an appreciative Seattle audience as she shared about the love and losses in her own life. By giving me that greatest gift, my friends have granted me the pleasure of knowing them in ways I wouldn't have otherwise. Susan Berlin's story reminded me that everyone has stories to tell, that dolls hold a power that time doesn't diminish. The dolls have reminded me that our human need and love for them is as natural as a bird building its nest. My friends have demonstrated the richness of stories that can be heard at our own kitchen tables. Through their endearing stories and photographs, it is my honor and delight to share the gift of my friends with you.

Carolyn Michael

Photo: Chelsea Balentine and dolls she made in Signe Feeney's third grade class at Margaret McKenny Elementary in Olympia, Washington.
Signe Feeney, photographer.

Susan Berlin

Who Would I Tell?

Who Would I Tell?

I didn't love my mother. We were too different and she had resolved her quandaries in ways that made it impossible for her to try to know me. She refused to defend me – against bullies, against teachers, against my father – expecting me to accept victimization as she had done. "Comb your hair," she'd say. "Smile."

I hated her passivity. "Why do you let Mrs. Levine talk to you on the phone all the time if you don't like her?" I would ask when I was small. When I was older, I'd snap "Mother! How can you let that con-man cheat you so badly and make you pay *him* for taking down the barn, when you know he's going to sell the wood and make a mint?" Later still, trying in my busy life to look after my elderly mother, I'd ask, "Did you remember to ask the doctor about your eyes?" She'd say, "Yes, but I didn't really understand what he told me." "Well, why didn't you ask him to explain it again?" "Dear, he's a very busy man, you know." And I'd explode in exasperation.

It wasn't till she was very old that she told me the story about her doll.

My grandfather was a tailor, something of a dreamer, a good designer but not a good businessman. For most of my mother's childhood, the family lived in a series of cold-water flats, the children sleeping four to a bed, the boarder given the only bedroom for the sake of his three dollars a week rent (which included my grandmother's cooking and laundry services) and the parents using the parlour as bedroom by night and workroom by day.

My mother went to school, where she learned about the American Dream and the vital importance of having a clean handkerchief pinned to your jumper every day. At home, as the oldest girl, she was the family drudge, and she also ran errands for her father, picking up fabric and delivering finished garments. Her world was limited, her dreams vast. She told me that she had been sure, in those days, that rich little girls could wear beautiful silk dresses when *they* scrubbed the floor.

One day, a customer came to the flat to pick up her finished coat. When she'd paid for it, she gave my grandfather a long, gray cardboard box. "For your little girl," she said.

At eighty-seven, telling me the story, my mother's eyes shone. "It was the only real doll I ever had, and she was beautiful. Long golden curls, a jointed body of papier-mache, a velvet dress with a lace collar. I would take her out of her box, hold her in my lap, stroke her hair. Every night, I put her back in her box, on top of the closet, so none of the younger children could get her and maybe break her."

One morning my mother's little sister got sick. In those days, in crowded, jostling, unsanitary slums, children died of mysterious illnesses: agues, fevers, summer dysentery. The baby was sick, fretful, crying. Anything to calm her, to cool her fever, to stave off terrible fears.

"Yetta, be a good girl. Let the baby play with your doll. You're a big girl. You're in school all day anyway and she's crying for the doll."

"No! It's my doll! She'll break it!"

"I won't let her break it. I'll watch her every minute."

"You can't, you're busy. Promise me – promise me you won't give her my doll."

"What kind of a sister are you, anyway? A selfish thing, that's what you are. Go, go off to school. You're late."

"Promise me!"

My grandmother gave the doll to the baby, swept the floor, boiled the laundry, hung the wash, started soup for supper. My mother came home from school. Her little sister had put the doll into the washbasin to bathe her. The jointed papiermache body, having soaked since early morning, collapsed as my mother seized it in rescue.

"You have to forgive her," her own mother said. "She's only a baby."

I was stabbed with pity. "What an awful story," I said. Something in her manner pushed me on. "You've never told me that story before."

"No," she said. "I never told anyone."

"No one? Never, in all these years?"

"No," she said looking at me in surprise. "Who would I have told it to?"

～

Susan Berlin is a writer, editor, community planner, handspinner and knitwear designer. She lives off-grid on one of the beautiful Canadian Gulf Islands with two cats and a Bernese Mountain dog and is enjoying the comfort of being one of the island's many eccentrics.

I met Susan in 1993 at the writing retreat where I first heard and was inspired by this story.

Photo: Susan's mother, Henrietta, and her little sister, Libby in 1905.

Vi (taqʷšəblu) Hilbert

I Wanted a Real Live Baby

I Wanted a Real Live Baby

My poor mother had eight pregnancies and I was the only one that survived. She lamented this condition of her loss but she and my dad poured all of their love and nurturing over me, their lone chick. My welfare was their primary concern. I should be protected from all danger. I would need to carry the responsibility of cultural knowledge, all of the inherited traditions. I must always conduct myself in a manner above reproach. Having instilled all of these rules to guide my mental, physical and emotional growth, I was given the lesson, loud and clear. Because they, my parents, had given me all of the guidelines for living in my world, I could now never do anything wrong. They, and the culture, had instructed me!

Oh, how I yearned for a sibling to share with. I envied all of my friends and relatives who had large families. My parents took me for overnight visits to many family gatherings. What a wonderful time it was to play with other young people – to hunt together, to explore the beaches and the woods together, to sing and pretend together. Lucky the families who had eight or ten children under one roof. As I voiced my wishes to belong to such families, the answer from them was always, "No, you are much luckier to be the only one. You can have everything for yourself, you don't have to wear hand-me-downs. You are the lucky one!"

To ease my loneliness, my mother would buy me doll after doll when she had a little money that could be spared. I kept telling her, "Mom, I don't want dolls. I want real live babies to hold and to love."

One time we were at a big summer gathering to celebrate some event together. This was a two or three day celebration, so my parents had set up camp. They had a tent for this purpose. Mother had feather beds and cooking gear for outdoors. This was always a very enjoyable time for all of us. Mother, however, was suffering from a very miserable abscessed tooth. She, who loved to visit and talk, was staying quietly in the tent, hoping to get some relief from her toothache.

Dad and I went our separate ways, visiting with our special friends. As I wandered around, I came upon one of our relatives. She was holding a baby. A baby! Oh, how wonderful. "May I hold it?" I pleaded.

"Yes, you may hold it. Do you want this baby?"

"Oh, yes! Oh, yes! Do you really mean that I can have it?"

"Yes, here are her diapers and her nursing bottles. She is yours!"

I was about ten years old and this baby was about six or seven months old. Gleefully, I walked my treasure back to the tent to show mother, My Baby!! I was bursting with happiness and pride. My real live baby.

I went into the tent. "Look, Mom, look at my baby."

"Your baby? What do you mean, *your* baby?"

"She is mine, Mama. The baby's mother gave her to me. See, here are her diapers and her bottles."

"Where is her mother?"

"She's gone. She gave me the baby and these things and she got into a car and left!"

"Oh, that crazy thing. Leave it to her to do something like that when here I am suffering with this toothache."

"That's all right, Mama. I'll take care of my baby!"

My parents raised my baby who grew up to have many babies of her own. I have not been able to keep in touch with her for all of these years but she did bring our family lots of happiness when she was our baby!

I could never do anything wrong!

~

Vi (taqʷšəblu) Hilbert is a great-grandmother and elder of the Upper Skagit Tribe of northern Puget Sound. As founder and director of Lushootseed Research, she has devoted her life to teaching and preserving the language (Lushootseed), literature and culture of her people. Among the numerous honors she has received for her work are the National Endowment for the Arts Ethnic Heritage Award and being named a Living Treasure of Washington State. She shares the ancient wisdom of her ancestors around the world and received a lifetime achievement award from NAPPS (National Association for the Preservation and Perpetuation of Storytelling). She lives in Seattle with her husband Don.

I met Vi in 1987 when I was teaching kindergarten in Seattle. A search for knowledge of the First People of the land where I live led me to Vi's dining room table, which happened to be just minutes from my own. She welcomed me into her huge extended Lushootseed family. Several of the stories in this book are by friends I met through Vi and her always open heart and door.

Photos: Vi with her parents Charley and Louise Anderson, 1940.
Dolls made by Vi Hilbert more than thirty years ago.

Lois Schluter

A Doll to Remember

A Doll to Remember

The doll I remember most vividly was not an ordinary doll, not beautiful and she had no name. She was my Indian doll, with an aged, shriveled face and long braids, wrapped in a blanket. Shapeless. Her arms and legs were immovable, her eyes black and penetrating. She was the kind of doll tourists buy. I treasure a photograph that captures for me the memory of this special doll from half a century ago. There's my Dad, looking so handsome and splendid in his Navy uniform and me in my dress with the tiny red hearts on the bodice – a picture to remind me of a memorable day, a rare moment shared with my father.

His visits were few with very long gaps between, but this was one of those times I was able to share with him. It was our day together. I was only five and he, of course, took me to the places that he was most familiar and comfortable with in Seattle, his stomping grounds in the heart of the city on First and Second Avenue. Even in 1943, it was a rough part of town, but it was a lively and popular place frequented by soldiers and sailors on leave.

I have fading memories of the live theater show my father chose for us. There was live music played on a tinny-sounding piano. Carnival-like entertainers were dressed in gaudy, colorful costumes. It wasn't exactly top-notch entertainment, but he took me where he thought a child would have fun watching jugglers and acrobats. Afterwards, he proudly introduced me to some of his best buddies and I felt very special, so proud to be his daughter.

Then my father did the most unusual thing. We slipped into a souvenir shop nestled between a pawn shop and an incredibly noisy tavern. There was the unmistakably sweet and pungent smell of cigars and tobacco. He bought me a gift. It was my Indian doll, and he had the photograph taken. The doll is long gone. I cannot remember when or where it disappeared. Yet I remember that day, the doll my father gave me and this often faraway, wonderful father I had.

~

Lois Schluter is a recently retired college counselor, storyteller, mother and grandmother. She lives near Bow, Washington, with her husband Walter. Lois is an enrolled member of Washington's Nooksack tribe. Her father, Percy Woodcock, was a Quinault. Lois is the only daughter of Vi (taqʷšəblu) Hilbert, an Upper Skagit elder.

I met Lois at a backyard salmon bake at Vi's where her blueberry tarts gave testament to Lois' fame as a gourmet cook. We discovered a mutual fondness for rocks and laughing uncontrollably.

Photo: Lois, her dad Percy Woodcock and her special doll.

Robert Rudine

Bawl Room Dance

Bawl Room Dance

A Writing Practice

The first exercise was to breathe a deep breath and write a word or phrase after each exhalation:

starry

fair

Corvette go-cart

dancing footed doll

disney

dizzy

1957

second place

tears

bawl room dance

room painted chocolate

parted on the left

1st grade specs

nearsighted

The next session was a three minute 'write' without pause; the 'trigger' was: "All by itself the screen began to glow...."

All by itself the screen began to glow. I'd cussed that damned computer, booting up so slow from every shutdown – shut me out – make simple acts complex, give me a complex, too; but, here the freaking thing was rebooting on its own. Thing is really scary. Why does it even need me? And then I realized I was asleep and I was really going to get a message from my deep unconscious, as willful and unknown as an artificial intelligence. I typed in the words: starry, fair, dappled, dizzy, disney, club footed, near-sighted…then, living doll.

Living Doll glowed on the screen and then I could see her mop-like hair and remember the night she invited me to dance – the lover I would have spurned – my booby prize princess.

It was 1957, the night of my very first school fair. I was in the first grade. Funny, it's as if my parents weren't there. It was magical…I blended….

Then we wrote for eight minutes, the trigger being: "The eyes of the doll...."

The eyes of the doll…were they little sightless patches of embroidery, speaking of nimble factory fingers waiting for the whistle to finally blow the blinders off of everyone and everything that put her behind the workbench, arthritis screaming up the carpal tunnel like a runaway freight in a bat blind cave? Were they like mine, nearsighted eyes half drowned in tears of disappointment?…Rosebud eyes crying for the lost Corvette go-cart, coveted raffle prize and not this club-footed princess booby prize that I danced with in the middle of the night in my room painted chocolate.

I had my raffle ticket. The lights were dazzling – turned the Walnut Hill Elementary School playground into a Disneyland to my first grade eyes. I felt like a winner. The corvette go-cart was perched seductively aslant like a rakish cap under a string of 60 watt bulbs. Texas heat, the only air I'd ever breathed, drank with sweat as sticky as Dr. Pepper's. In my mind's eye, I could see the sequined models who showed off the 1958 models at the Great State Fair of Texas. Maybe I was just nearsighted…I was seeing the girls' prize – a dancing doll. She was first-grade-life-size, had mop hair and red shoes with white elastic bands to wrap around the feet of her dance partner. Some little girl would be lucky.

My name was in the pot a lot. I sold tickets to all my neighbors for this Frontier Day's Celebration. My parents bought a half dozen. I had on my cowboy outfit, probably with my six shooter. Each stub (like a bullet) had my name on it.

Carolyn wouldn't tell us how long the last session was and I went a sentence or two over the bell. The trigger was: "I had this doll…."

I had this doll to my shame, my shame. "Robby is a boy's name! How could you give me a doll? I won the Corvette, didn't I?"

"No, Robby, you won the second prize; it's a dancing doll. Boys dance with girls and so this is a doll for a boy," my mother soothed.

"There's no such thing as a doll for a boy!" I sobbed.

I wanted more than anything to jump onto that 1958 Corvette go-cart (just a smaller version of the one I'd seen at the State Fair), holster my six-shooter and rumble flat out onto the blacktop of Walnut Hill Lane laying smoking rubber as far away as I could get from that school, as far away from home, as far from Big "D" where they laughed that "Robby won a doll"…head out on Route 66 as far as I could go.

"But, Robby is a boy's name!" I screamed. I left all right. It must have spoiled the prize ceremony a bit to see the little cowboy be such a poor winner when he was handed his life-size dance pardner. She swooned into his arms as the parent dragged him, inconsolable, away to his home.

I can't remember ever crying any more than that night in my room painted chocolate. Even my younger brother had the sense to leave me alone. My older sister tried to say something complimentary about my doll and I'd swung at her.

Still, in the middle of the night, all alone, all cried out, I slipped those stretchy elastic bands over my pajama feet and we danced. She let me lead and it seemed for all the world that the only one who understood was my mop hair girl who wasn't even embarrassed that I'd cried for shame at being shotgun wed to her. She just seemed to let me be. I hated her, wanted to hit her, but I clung to her and did a sad Texas waltz in my room painted chocolate.

Then, I sat down on my bed and unhooked her feet from mine, brushed my teeth and went to bed strangely sad and comforted and exhausted. We never danced again. And I don't know but my mother must have spirited the life-size dancing doll out of the house from her under-my-bed exile and probably gave her to some lucky girl and she danced all her nights by the light of the moon. And still she was the only doll that was ever really all my own.

~

Robert Rudine, born May 16, 1951, in Florence Nightingale Hospital in Dallas, Texas, was gifted every one of his young years with a complete cowboy outfit. His Dallas dances with dolls days are long gone. Now also a member of the Lushootseed Family, he resides on the small island nation of Tui Tui entirely surrounded by Lake Union's Seattle with his wife Janet Yoder, their hound Saba, and a collection of dolls made by his grandmother.

I first met Robby in Vi Hilbert's back yard and became acquainted with his sense of humor and knack for squeezing the most out of life.

Editor's note: On one of the evenings friends gathered at my home to write together, Robby Rudine came, hoping to move his story beyond staring at a blank computer screen. Inspired by Natalie Goldberg's* technique of writing practice, the four of us each put a word or phrase on a piece of paper to be drawn and used as a "trigger." The idea was to write without stopping for the designated writing time. After each round of writing, we'd read aloud what we wrote, then go on to the next round. No comments were made until the end of the evening. As Robby was leaving, I asked him to consider submitting his story unedited, just as it had unfolded. I thought it would give readers a unique glimpse into his writing process as well as delightfully convey his story. He looked at me askance but after a few days consideration, he obliged.

"Bawl Room Dance" is Robby's writing practice.

*Natalie Goldberg is the author of Writing Down the Bones and several other books.

Photo: Cowboy Robby and his Cowgirl sister, Francine.

Janet Yoder

George Rufus Yoder

George Rufus Yoder

He joined our family at Christmas, though only Santa witnessed his actual arrival. By early morning he sat on the hearth in front of Karen's stocking, a Charley McCarthy puppet doll. He sported beige pants, a white shirt, a red plaid jacket so loud you could hear it across the room, and a classic bow tie. He was a dressy guy with a big smiley mouth just aching to open up and talk.

Karen didn't take to him immediately. Maybe she'd set her Santa sights on something more feminine, a lovely creature in a fairy dress of pink gauze sprinkled with glitter. Instead she got a soft-bodied, hard headed guy whose lower jaw moved when you tugged on the string coming out the back of his neck. Karen pulled the string and waited like she expected a recorded message, "I'm hungry" or "I'm wet." But no sound came. George hadn't gotten his voice yet. He wasn't even George yet. I suppose at that point, he could have become someone other than George, though it's hard to imagine.

He came to life in Gail's hands, spoke right up in a nasal voice. "Hiya, hiya, hiya. Name's George. Put her there." He reached out a firm plastic hand to shake with family members. Karen looked annoyed that her Santa gift had just named himself and not even while she was holding him.

Once he started talking, there was no stopping him. His voice came out the same no matter which of us four girls was his handler. Not that George could really be handled.

"Hey lady, what's for supper?" he'd ask Mom, leaning back and crossing one soft leg over the other with a look of nonchalance. Mom answered him, "Chicken and mashed potatoes" or "Meat loaf and carrot salad." Everyone answered him, responding almost involuntarily to that insistent voice. Well, everyone but Dad. He held back while the rest of us talked as much to George as we did to each other. Suddenly a whole lot more talking was going on in our house.

"He's just a dummy," said Dad. The word dummy sent George into apoplectic fits. He waved both plaid arms and stomped his feet. "I'm no dummy. I'm a genius. Jeeeenyus!" He stretched the word out for emphasis, turning it into a refrain as powerful as the Hallelujah Chorus. Even total strangers who innocently referred to George as a dummy got the full response. George did not let anyone get away with using the D word to describe him.

George addressed Dad as, "Hey, mister" and asked him lots of questions. "Can we go out for root beer floats?" "Can we stay up and watch Man from U.N.C.L.E.?"

"Tell that dummy not to talk so much," said Dad.

"I'm a genius," insisted George.

"He's a dummy." Dad had to speak carefully so he wouldn't say "You're a dummy." That would mean he was talking directly to George, acknowledging him, engaging him in a dialog. If Dad believed George was a dummy and Dad talked to George, then what did that make Dad? The rest of us just accepted that George was a genius.

George's personality became more irreverent as time went by, some quirky combination we four sisters gave him. In Becky's hands, George ran his plastic hand through his plastic hair, saying "I'm handsome. I'm dapper." With Gail, he blithely talked to total strangers, usually getting wonderfully gratifying responses. He snickered a lot when Karen held him, and I'm pretty sure a few snide remarks slipped out of his mouth when I pulled his string.

George had lots to say and sometimes we had to wait in line to get a chance to pull his vocal string. "You've had him all morning." "He's mine. I got him for Christmas." But it was too late for George to be claimed by any one person. His personality had already expanded beyond that and kept getting larger, more complete. He was becoming the brother we never had. He even got into sibling squabbles. Once he and Karen were so mad at each other that George kicked her with one of his very solid, real leather wing tips, bruising her shin and her feelings. George had to make heartfelt apologies to get back in her good graces.

He started using his full name around that time – George Rufus Yoder. I don't remember where the Rufus came from, but, like the wing tips, the name rounded him out, giving his character complete and irreversible distinction.

George liked to go places. He started riding with us in the car, sitting in the back seat, always moving his jaw as the car rolled along. The lower portion of his mouth clapped into the upper as if he were applauding his own words, slapping exclamation points onto the end of each statement.

We took him to the Bon Marche store at the brand new mall. A woman there smiled at George and said, "What a handsome guy." "Thank you," George replied. "And polite too," the woman continued before stepping onto our town's first escalator. George's ego was truly fattened by this experience. He went home repeating "I'm handsome and polite" as if it were a mantra that brought him all he needed.

"I wish you wouldn't take him everywhere," Dad said. But we did. We took him on our summer evening drives around the orchards, seeing how plump the peaches and apricots were and later the pears and all varieties of apples. George learned their names: Jonathans, Macintosh, Goldens, Transparents. "Pretty good-looking apples if you go in for that sort of thing," George said. "Now me," he pointed a plastic hand at his red plaid chest, "I'm a candy bar kind of guy, mainly Snickers. Ha, ha."

George often sang in the car and it was always the same song. "Oh when those cotton fields get rotten, you don't get very much cotton. In them old cotton fields back home." It went on and on. I'm not sure why that song became George's but it did. Maybe it was because his body was stuffed with wads of cotton, that cotton was his very flesh, therefore the cotton fields were his ancient home. And what would happen to George if his cotton got rotten? Perhaps he was speculating on all that or else just belting out the only song he knew.

"Can't you make him be quiet?" Dad asked from the front seat. But it was too late for George to be quiet. Quiet was not in George's nature. "He's becoming your alter ego," Dad said. "Do you know what that means?"

We may not have all four known what that meant but George did. "Walter Eagle," he shouted. "I'm your Walter Eagle." Then he laughed, we laughed, and even Dad might have smiled.

Dad was right. George had become an alter ego for four girls. He was able to give voice to every less-than-correct and less-than-polite thing we might be thinking. George could say anything, things girls couldn't or shouldn't say, and he said them in a loud self-confident voice. He activated some part of all of us, bringing the family to life in ways we couldn't have imagined prior to his arrival.

Dad's resistance was part of George's challenge. But when Dad got us lost in some strange town on the way to somewhere at the end of a long day on the road, family members started to grump at him. But not George. "Hey, mister, you must know the secret back road to where we're going, right?" George released the travel tension through his smiley plastic mouth that never stopped flapping.

Family vacations were prime time for George. He talked to the man at the toll booth where the Vernita Bridge crossed the Columbia, a crossing we had to make on the way to anywhere. "Hiya mister. How're ya doing?" George waved a plastic hand at the man as Dad grabbed his change and stepped on the gas.

"I don't want him talking to strangers," Dad said. It was interesting that he didn't know which kid to blame, only George. "I especially don't want him talking when we cross the border into Canada. We could get in trouble if he talks there."

So George sat quietly in the back seat while the uniformed border guard asked Dad where we were going, for how long, and where we lived. The guard concentrated on us, tapped a pen on a clipboard, emphasizing his job of protecting Canada from the likes of us. Then his eyes landed on George. His lips moved a little like they might think about smiling some time. "That a family member?" he asked.

"Yes," said George. "I'm a genius."

"Have a nice vacation." The guard waved us across onto Canadian soil, George's first trip out of the country.

"I'm a family member," said George. Dad groaned from the driver's seat and muttered something about creating a monster. But George didn't hear. He'd launched into another full-voiced round of cotton balls getting rotten in them old cotton fields back home.

George's mouth was his major organ. It was a moving part, operated by a string that came out the back of his neck. It was a big mouth that clacked each time it opened and closed. The mouth could move pretty fast but never as fast as the words tumbling out of him. He could get two or three syllables out for every smack of plastic against plastic, quite an accomplishment. Maybe George was the real ventriloquist, able to talk with a minimum of moves, though his moves were as large and overstated as his personality or his plaid jacket.

In later years, George's mouth was the subject of medical attention. The worst of all ailments befell him – lockjaw. His jaw opened when his string was pulled, but refused to snap back into place when the string was released. Instead his lower jaw hung there, leaving his mouth unnaturally wide open, not the most impressive pose for a genius to strike. George had to use his hand to push his jaw shut after each opening. "Oh no," he moaned, "I've got lockjaw."

George went through a depression during this time. No one held him or pulled his string. He took to lying around all day on the sofa with his jaw open, looking perpetually surprised or ready to speak. But he spoke very little. The whole family became quiet during this time, each member distracted, turned inward, not able to sit around and jaw together as usual.

Finally George submitted to surgery. Doctor Mom used a kitchen knife to reach down between George's lips and teeth, way back into the plastic cavity of his head. I couldn't see what she did, but it worked. "Hey, that's more like it. I can talk, I can talk!" The patient crowed like a rooster that had slept through the entire winter, snapping back to life with renewed vigor and much jaw action. He'd been saving up a lot of things to say during his ailment. Turns out we all had.

George continued to grow and change. During the hippie era, he donned a pair of leather moccasins with fringe strings hanging down the sides. He took to wearing a wig, a fall actually, of long straight hair that hid his plastic ears and hung down over the shoulders of his red plaid jacket, which by that time was only a background for the vast display of George's political buttons. His messages ran the gamut: "Shirley Chisolm for President," "We try harder," "Make Love not War," "Save the Whales," and a peace sign.

George's vocabulary mellowed. "Cool," he said, nodding his head to music only he heard. "Far out, man." "Groovy." If his plastic fingers could have separated, he would no doubt have flashed the peace sign at all comers.

George's hippie phase lasted a year or so. Then one day the wing tips miraculously re-appeared and his hair returned to the trim held-in-place look. His cheeks appeared rosy and plump again now that the long hair no longer hid his face. He stopped being mellow and returned to his original boisterous self. I think we were all relieved to have the old George back.

That's the way it was with George. He became part of us, changed as we did, and ex-pressed things for us. He complained, praised, enthused, spoke out every thought, sang loudly about cotton fields, never mind that he had never seen one. Nothing stopped him from belting it out. He was not a shy guy. He liked himself, thought he was hand-some, dapper, a genius, a fun guy, a cool dude, the life of the party. George had self-esteem back before it was in vogue. He must have bathed in the stuff, soaked it in through every cotton and plastic pore. He had so much that when we held him in our laps and operated his jaw, some of it rubbed off on us.

But it still got to George that Dad never directly acknowledged him. Oh, I don't mean he moaned and groaned about it, but you could tell he was waiting to hear from Dad. Finally, inevitably, he did. Dad went down to Tennessee on a business trip. During his absence the mailman brought a postcard addressed to George Rufus Yoder. The picture showed a cotton field ready to harvest, every plant bursting with cotton balls. A plastic bag stapled to the card contained real live raw cotton. The message read, "To George. You'll be happy to know the cotton's not rotten."

George's face seemed to take on a glow. "See my postcard," he held it up for each of us to see. "It's from the mister." He read the words aloud repeatedly, patting the cotton balls with his hand. Then he looked around the living room like he belonged to all of us. And he did.

~

Janet Yoder lives in Seattle and LaConner with her husband Robby Rudine and dog Saba. She is honored to be part of the Lushootseed Family centered around Vi Hilbert. She visits George Rufus Yoder from time to time at his home in Wenatchee. Even though his jaw barely moves now, after a few minutes in the arms of one of the sisters, George still miraculously becomes as talkative and opinionated as ever. Naturally his opinion of himself remains quite high.

I met Janet in Vi Hilbert's back yard. Months later we discovered we are connected not only by our inclusion in the Lushootseed Family but by marriage. Her sister Gail is married to a distant cousin of mine.

Photos: George Rufus Yoder. Kari Berger, photographer.

Karen Yoder

Playing Hooky with George

Playing Hooky with George

Not all of my memories of George are fond, like the time he kicked me with his wing tip shoes. It really hurt! But here I include one of my favorite memories of him.

When I was little, I was dyslexic which meant it was really hard for me to learn to read or write. My kindergarten teacher told everyone at a PTA meeting that I was retarded. All the kids in class found out, which meant that for the next ten years of my life I was the laughingstock at school.

I hated school. Mom understood this so she let me miss sometimes. She said I had "a touch of the flu" which meant I could stay home all day, eat soda crackers, drink 7-up and lie around on the couch watching old "I Love Lucy" and "Andy of Mayberry" reruns.

One day Gail and George had "a touch of the flu" too. We were sitting around watching Jack LaLaine. Gail helped George go through all of Jack's exercises. Jack said, "Inhale!" George inhaled. Jack said, "Exhale!" George obeyed. Jack and George continued to inhale and exhale while stretching their arms up, then releasing them down.

Finally after the last "Inhale," Jack went on to demonstrate a different exercise where you put a broomstick behind your shoulders and twisted back and forth. George continued to inhale. He inhaled as deeply as he could. He started to turn blue in his plastic face. Finally George started yelling, "But, Jack, hey Jack buddy, when can I exhale?"

George was fun and made you laugh. I'd love to see him again.

~

Karen Yoder was born and raised in eastern Washington State. After studying dance for several years in Seattle, she moved to Madrid, Spain, to study flamenco. She has lived in Spain for many years, where she works as a flamenco dancer and part-time English teacher. She lives in the village of La Font d'en Carros in Valencia Province with her husband Antonio and their daughter Tania who loves to play with Barbies and stuffed animals.

I met Karen at Janet Yoder and Robby Rudine's houseboat one 4th of July when she danced for everyone gathered. Karen and Janet are sisters.

Photos: The Yoder family: Elsie, Janet, Bob (holding Karen), Becky & Gail.
Karen getting reacquainted with George.

Dana Gilbert

George and Georgina

[signature: Dana Gilbert]

George and Georgina

Hi, my name is Dana Gilbert. I love George and Georgina! My mom (Gail) loves them too! When my mom was a little girl Karen,(my mom's sister), got George for Christmas. But my mom loved him so much she took him! The whole family loved him, except my grandpa Bob. When my mom's parents had an anniversary Janet, Becky, Gail,and Karen got them an other doll, Georgina! When I was 4, George and Georgina sat ontop of a net above my bed, and one night they fell on me,and boy did they hurt!!!

My friend Camie just read a book called "Night of the Living Dummy" and we found George, who looked just like the one on the cover of the book, and it scared us!

I'm 9 years old.

I saw an "I Love Lucy" about Dummies!

Bye. Your friend

Dana Gilbert

Dana Gilbert, a few years older now, is in eighth grade in Wenatchee, Washington. She loves to act, dance, and play her clarinet. She also enjoys hanging with her friends and playing fast pitch softball. She has performed in "The Short Shakespeareans" for four years and played numerous roles in other plays as well.

I met Dana through her aunt, Janet Yoder, and became reacquainted with her Dad, Kevin, whom I hadn't seen since he was a little boy. Kevin and I always knew we were cousins of some kind, so I finally traced the connection. Our great-grandmothers were sisters.

Photo: Dana with Georgina, Grandma Elsie Yoder, and mother Gail with George.
Drawing by Dana Gilbert.

Jay Miller

My Teddy Bear Slipped and Drowned

My Teddy Bear Slipped and Drowned

Small, white, fuzzy – my one and only teddy bear drowned. Some details are vague with the years, but others continue to haunt me.

In the Southwest, the native Pueblos have a custom in which the spirits called kachinas come every spring to bring rain for the fields and gifts to the children. A boy will get a wooden bow and arrows and a girl will get a carved wooden doll that looks like one of these kachinas. Woe to anyone visiting the pueblo when the boys get up on the flat roofs with their new bows. Arrows have a way of raining down until they are all gone.

I suppose it was this custom that made me aware that, while I must have had action figures of some kind to play with, I had no dolls as such nor was I likely to have any. Among my neighbors, however, were two girls who had lots of dolls. When we played together, their dolls came along into the fields and arroyos.

One day, my friend had a tiny, white, fuzzy teddy bear that she gave to me. It was small enough to carry around tucked into my pocket so that the head and outstretched arms stuck out. He went everywhere with me until it became clear that he would get very dirty, so then he stayed in my room, only coming out occasionally.

When school was out and summer began, the plan was for neighborhood kids to sleep outside in tents. My backyard was where the boys would stay. Someone had a copy of a cub scout handbook and we all read about camping. The funny thing is that the handbook was, I realize now, obviously written for kids outside the Southwest. It told how you should dig a trench around your tent so the rain would run off to keep the insides dry. Where I lived, it was dry all the time except for flash floods during spring thunderstorms. That was the reason we could not play in the dry creek beds. Any moment a rainstorm from far away, farther than you could see or know about, could send a torrent of water raging down the channel. Now, of course, the Army Corps of Engineers has built huge concrete flood control dams and runoffs to save children and the land from this fate.

Anyway, we set up our tent, probably with the help of some parent. We moved sleeping bags, pillows, and flashlights inside. We were staying for the duration.

Then, to be sure, we got trenching tools – some old army-surplus folding shovels painted olive drab. We dug a trench all around our tent and made a downhill runoff. We worked long and hard. We dug sand, mind you, and sand drains very well all by itself. But we did what the book said to do. We were in league with cub scouts everywhere.

That night we could hardly wait to move into our tent. We planned to be up all night talking and goofing around. We were on our own. We were big. Of course, from all the work, we were also exhausted and went right to sleep.

In the morning we went into the house to eat and to use the bathroom. We had not yet learned to appreciate camping without any amenities at all.

Every night we slept in our tent. Sometimes animals came into the yard to add excitement, but mostly summer nights in the tent became routine. Somewhere along the way, my teddy bear moved into the tent. He stayed there during the day and slept there at night, sharing my sleeping bag. Because he was inside, he did not get dirty.

One night, as happened rarely but dramatically, there was a thunder and lightning storm. I am sure that we had to convince our parents to let us stay out in the tent, but we did. We talked about how effective our trench would be at keeping us dry.

The rains came. Lightning lit up the sky, even inside the tent. Thunder rumbled near and far. We were snug, dry, and warm. It was a hot night, after all. We slept late in the morning because we were up most of the night.

When I went to leave teddy in the tent, he was gone. I turned over and turned out my sleeping bag, then everyone else's. I ransacked the tent. Nothing.

I went outside. I walked around the tent. I walked around it again. I got on my hands and knees. Then, like a scene in a horror film, I saw a glint of white in a lump of sand at the bottom of the trench. I picked up the soggy lump and watched as gobs of sand plopped off. What was left had the limp shape of my teddy bear.

I ran for help. My mother took one look and said there was no way to clean up teddy. He was gone for good. No, I pleaded. Surely we could dry him out, brush him off, and wash him thoroughly. To her credit, my mother let me try. I left teddy on a rock in the sun.

He dried stiff. I brushed him off. He was a sick brownish tinge. I never washed him because I left him out in the sun again and he somehow disappeared. I have no memory that he was ever formally buried, thrown out or sent away. I only know that he was gone at some point and I became occupied with other activities.

As an adult, I realize that white, fuzzy stuffed animals are very impractical if they lead lives that are at all active. I now suspect that I both received and lost teddy because of his active life. Because there were no formal good-byes, however, I know that he is still around somewhere. I hope it is dry, warm and sunny so he can enjoy himself to the fullest and never have to worry about rain, lightning, thunder or deep trenches.

By the way, I now have kachina dolls of my own.

~

Jay Miller is mostly over his teddy bear trauma. He lives in Seattle where he enjoys hiking in the mountains, kayaking along shores, and eating salmon and pies as much as writing and teaching in the US and Canada. He is the author of six books and numerous publications based on research throughout North America, particularly among New Mexico Pueblos, Oklahoma Delawares, British Columbia Tsimshian, Washington State Salishans, Nevada Numic, Oklahoma Creek (Mvskogee), Oklahoma Caddo, Ontario Ojibwa, and Wisconsin Menomini. All of these nations cherish and encourage the use of dolls by people of all ages.

I met Jay while feasting on salmon at one of the many gatherings at Vi and Don Hilbert's home.

Photo: Jay with a possible relative to his original small, white, fuzzy teddy bear. Carolyn Michael, photographer

Carol Severance

Plastic Piano Keys

Plastic Piano Keys

My Mom liked nothing better than making children happy, her own and everyone else's. Her home was filled with toys and her heart was filled with laughter. She shared both freely.

Christmas was always a special time for Mom and she did her best to make each one memorable. My favorite took place when I was eight. Under the tree I found a beautiful doll and a whole suitcase full of doll clothes. Mom had sewn the clothes herself, using left-over pieces of fabric and lace, buttons and ribbons from her vast collection of such things.

There was a blue dress that matched Dad's new shirt, and a skirt of the same cloth as my brother's Christmas trousers. There were outfits that matched my own, and others that looked just like Mom's. Long dresses, short dresses, ruffled, straight, beaded dresses, hats and slippers and petticoats – each had some bit of fabric or trim connected to our family, our house, our friends. There was a shirt like the kitchen curtains and a tiny fur cape made from a hat I had worn as an infant.

When my sister was eight, Mom and I worked together to sew her a big box of clothes to go with her Christmas doll. I remember hand-beading the bodice of a frilly pink dress and stitching lace to the underskirt of another. Eventually, Mary passed on her doll and its well-worn wardrobe to her daughter Annie.

My doll had disappeared by the time my own daughter Linina turned eight. So I found a new one and, like my mother, created a wardrobe from remnants to go with it. Dresses, blouses and coats matched clothes that she, her father and brother and I wore. Linina played with that doll well into her teens and today shares it with her Little Sister, Latoyia.

It was always my mother's pleasure to recall those special dolls as well as the other toys and games our family shared. She continued to gift us with toys even after we were grown. Whenever I visited her in her later years – which was never often enough as we were separated by thousands of miles – Mom and I made at least one trip to a toy store. We wandered the aisles together, driving toy cars and trucks while making motor sounds with our mouths and laughing at our silliness. We played miniature pianos, beat on tinny-sounding xylophones and petted all the stuffed animals.

"Do you remember that suitcase full of doll clothes you had when you were little?" Mom always asked when we reached the dolls.

"That was my favorite Christmas, Mom," I always replied, and we would laughingly retell the story of that special gift.

As we spoke, Mom would reach out to lift the edge of a tiny skirt or peek inside a baby doll's jacket. Some outfits brought the hint of a frown, not quite living up to her standards of construction. Others brought nods of satisfaction. Well-made or not, each bit of clothing was smoothed carefully back into place by loving fingertips.

Eventually, Mom's memory began to fail. The silent encroachment of Alzheimer's disease fragmented her thoughts while memories of both past and present began to dissolve. Faces, conversations, birthday parties, even Christmases disappeared from Mom's conscious mind almost as quickly as they occurred.

Still, whenever we visited a toy store, she would reach out to touch the doll clothes and ask, "Do you remember that suitcase full of doll clothes you had when you were little?"

My answer was always the same, and the retelling of that tale always brought her a smile.

When Mom died, her family and friends gathered to celebrate her life, then sent her on her way surrounded by colorful toys.

Afterwards, I returned home and began to sew.

Like Mom, I have over the years accumulated a closet full of fabric remnants and buttons and ribbons, some directly transplanted from hers. There will be grandchildren someday, I thought. How better to share their Great Grandma Dorothy with them than through a big box full of doll clothes? Like the ones Mom made years before, each of these little dresses or shirts or skirts would have a connection to some part of our family's history.

When my eight-year-old niece Elena came to visit, she was surprised by my new doll and its dozen or so outfits, and delighted to be allowed to play with them. She dressed and redressed the doll, pausing to inspect each of the little dresses and skirts carefully. She ran her fingers across the lace and ribbons, poked at beads and buttons. She peeked under the skirts and inside the jackets, just like Mom had done.

So, of course, I went back to the toy store.

As I stood choosing a doll for Elena, I heard laughter from the next aisle. It reminded me of my Mom and an image flashed in my mind of the Salvation Army Giving Tree I had passed on my way into the mall. The tree was laden with paper stars carrying children's special holiday wishes and I recalled how much Mom had loved making Christmas special for her own children and everyone else's. I smiled and added six more dolls to my cart. The tinkling of plastic piano keys followed me from the store.

For the next few weeks, I cut and basted and sewed. Elena was thrilled with her doll, and when she learned of my plans for the others, she immediately offered to help. Together we assembled the dolls and their wardrobes and packaged them in special Christmas baskets. Then we delivered them to the mall where they were quickly spirited away to become part of six other little girls' Christmases.

The following year, Elena brought her good friend Rachel to help. The two girls packaged another six dolls for the Giving Tree and helped transport them as well. During the year other dolls, each with its own wardrobe, were distributed through the Red Cross and other agencies and individuals. A few dolls, dressed in special Hawaiian attire, were sold to help defray costs.

Friends and neighbors, even strangers, donated fabric and ribbons and lace. One lovely lady named Mary sent a package of buttons, lace and other trim that her own mother had used years ago to make doll clothes for her children and grandchildren. From now on, the Christmas wardrobes, as well as the others, will contain connections to a widely-extended family.

For her eighth birthday, I sent a doll to my great niece Samantha. Samantha is the eldest of her generation and remembers her Great Grandma Dorothy, so I included a small photo album with pictures of our mutual ancestors and current relatives along with the history of each of her new doll's outfits as they relate to our family. I also told her the story of her Great Grandma Dorothy's first Christmas doll so long ago.

My own collection of doll clothes continues to grow. There is a lacy pink gown made from remnants of Linina's prom dress and a vest and trousers that match one of her brother's shirts. There are hodgepodge outfits that include bits and pieces from the many gifts of fabric and buttons and ribbons and dresses and skirts that match those that have been given away. Each little outfit is special and each carries its own special story.

The ones I like best, and the ones that visiting children most often leave on the dolls, are those made from fabric and trim that came from Mom. Soft gingham and crisp dotted swiss, tiny buttons shaped like hearts, ribbons in myriad colors.

"That one came from your Great Grandma Dorothy," I'll tell my grandchildren someday. "She was a special lady. She liked to make little boys and girls happy."

On a recent visit to my daughter – which doesn't happen often enough as we are now separated by thousands of miles – Linina and I took our usual trip to the local toy store.

When we reached the dolls, I asked, "Do you remember that box of doll clothes you had when you were little?" I knew she did. The doll and its wardrobe were sitting in her guest room, surrounded by other toys.

Linina grinned and replied, "That was my favorite Christmas, Mom."

I peeked under the edge of a frilly little skirt, nodded in satisfaction, then we wandered off to play with the cars and trucks and to pet the stuffed animals. Laughter and the tinkling of plastic piano keys followed us from the store.

~

Carol Severance is a novelist and playwright with a special interest in Pacific Islands Peoples and their environments. She won science fiction's Compton Crook Award for best first novel for *Reefsong*. She and her husband Craig, a scholarly fisherman, live in Hawaii above Hilo Bay with an undetermined number of geckos.

My friendship with Carol began in Seattle the day Vi Hilbert introduced us and deepened during the time I made Hilo my home.

Photos: Carol's mother, Dorothy Wilcox.
Doll wearing Hawaiian attire created by Carol.

Annette Sumada

The Boys' Tree

The Boys' Tree

When our second son left Hawaii for university life on "the mainland," I was inspired to recreate special memories of our four sons for the family Christmas tree. I began a series of simple felt dolls, representing each son's hobbies and adventures, to be hung as tree ornaments.

The first dolls were of Rick, our third son, a talented football and basketball player at Hilo High School. It was fun capturing Ricky's sports memories by recreating his school's uniforms, including his Converse high-top sneakers and blue and gold socks. The rest of the family wanted to see themselves represented on the tree, so the tradition began.

For several years, I always had a new set of dolls of one or more of the boys ready for Christmas tree decorating. As our sons came home for Christmas vacation each year, it was one of their first surprises to see what memory their Mom had immortalized in an ornament doll. In time, the usual glass balls and tinsel decorations were replaced with a family of dolls in an "album of memories."

One year, I made dolls to depict the colleges each attended. John remembers the Christmas he made a surprise flight home for the holidays from the University of Washington with an eight-foot, freshly-cut Douglas Fir tree as luggage, perfect for hanging his purple and gold doll. Jiro Allen was attending the U. S. Air Force Academy. His Academy sweatshirts and oversized combat boots inspired the consummate airman warrior doll that protects the world against "communist aggression." Ricky appeared on the tree in crimson and gray as a Washington State Cougar. Don wore the University of Hawaii Rainbows t-shirt for his alma mater.

All the boys were active with sports and outdoor activities. Don's doll reminds him of his numerous medals won and the speed records he broke as a high school swimmer. Jiro and Ricky have Little League dolls to portray their stints with the Indians. Many summers John came home to enjoy fishing and spearing. He was especially successful in his multi-colored lucky swim trunks. During his vacation Jiro took time to learn a few boxing tips from his Uncle Tai Sun. After returning to the Academy, he put his Uncle's advice to good use and never got a black eye like the one sewed into his boxing doll. Rick, however, spent the summer as a house painter in Washington. It's doubtful he kept his overalls as clean as those his doll is wearing.

By far the most controversial doll is of Rick and his blanket. From age three to thirty-seven, Rick has slept with a special blanket affectionately referred to as his "wow-wow." Rick's wife, Carolyn, tolerates Rick's nighttime security blanket as long as he washes it once or twice a year. Prior to their marriage, the family warned her of Rick's traumatic experience when Mom washed his "wow-wow" without his knowledge and he found it had lost its special feel and comforting smell.

After these main dolls were completed, I fashioned a series of smaller dolls of the Sumada boys and their life in Hilo. From skateboarding and eating shave ice or watermelon to being in the Waiakea Intermediate School ukulele band, to high school graduation, few activities escaped becoming doll legend. Perhaps seeing dolls of the boys holding their pet rabbit and cat made the family dog Mitzi growl and demand a doll of her own on the tree.

The Boys' Tree became a big hit with their friends. Many wanted to be included, so they made dolls of their own to add to the collection. One girl made a swimmer wearing goggles and another made dolls of herself and Don holding hands. A friend who wasn't confident making figures fashioned Big Mac and fried egg ornaments. These continue to be a part of the family tree.

These ornaments have made Christmas very special for our family. My grandchildren now gather at our home to decorate the tree. They hang images of their fathers' growing-up years on the branches and scatter assorted old toys and stuffed animals between the branches and on the floor. Some day this album of memories will pass on to each of their homes, but until then, we will continue to enjoy the Boys' Tree as a special family tradition.

~

Annette Sumada spent many years as an elementary school teacher, but "retired" is not a word to describe her. She designs and makes award-winning Hawaiian quilts, paints watercolors on silk and gardens. She and her husband Mitsugu live in Hilo, Hawaii.

I met Annette in a Chinese brush-painting class taught by Hawaii artist, Jane Chao.

Photo: The Sumada family's tree ornaments.

Nina Munk

The Night My Fanny Hit the Wall

The Night My Fanny Hit the Wall

My dolls were possessed with life. I believed that within every cotton, polyester or plastic body there existed a heart, a heart which was capable of experiencing emotion – sadness, joy, anger. They were my children, an estimated thirty of them, and I did my best to mother them.

I was an extremely jealous child, always wanting my parents to donate more of their attention to me and less to my brother. Therefore, I was always very sensitive to my dolls' so-called "jealousies." I established a sleeping chart in which my dolls took turns on a rotational basis sleeping in my bed. Each night I visited the unlucky ones who were forced to sleep in a playpen and reassured them that I loved each and every one of them. When I crawled into my warm bed and snuggled with my "doll of the night," I felt a spark of guilt for abandoning the others. I worried that they were cold, or worse, angry with me. On cold windy nights I often covered them gently with a pink quilt from my bed.

One night during the summer of second grade, I sat on the yellow shag rug of my bedroom playing with three of my favorite dolls. Their names were Fanny Zia, Norris Lars and Fruitcake. Fanny Zia and I were practicing our acrobatic tricks by repeatedly jumping off my bed. For the grand finale, Fanny Zia and I did a 360 degree flip off the bed. I landed with a perfect 10, but Fanny unfortunately crashed into the wall. I peeked at my motionless child collapsed on the rug, her plastic face full with smile. Why must you smile? I wondered. I had only a single horrifying realization: My dolls, my darling children and best friends, were not alive. I held Fanny Zia close to my heart and began to cry.

～

Nina Munk, fifteen years old when she wrote her story, has grown a few inches since then and is a college sophomore. She currently resides in Seattle's Ballard district and writes country love songs for her family.

I met Nina at her home when I was visiting her mother, Ann Teplick, whom I'd met writing at a Seattle cafe. Nina introduced me to about two dozen of her old dolls and charmed me with countless stories of their relationships and adventures.

Photos: Nina with Fanny, Zia, Fruitcake, and Norris Lars.
Young Nina with Raggedy Ann.

Kari Berger

Tales from the Heart

Tales from the Heart

Dolls are for girls who like being girls – sissies. Dolls were given to me but I did not want to be a girl and was not going to be caught liking dolls. Baby dolls were especially repulsive.

Family Legend: Sometime in the 1890's in a poor fishing village in Scotland, my great-grand-mother Helen was pregnant with her fifth child. After four daughters, she and her husband Thomas wanted a son. When her husband drowned in Moray Firth, she named the unborn child after him. At birth the baby's name was changed to Thomasina. Helen raised her five daughters alone, all of them working hard to put bread on the table. Thomasina had one possession, which she dearly loved – her doll. One day her mother made her give the doll to someone less fortunate. Thomasina, my Granny, never forgave her.

I remember Granny rocking in her chair in a basement closet lit only by a grimy window surrounded by woolen coats, mothballs flavoring the stale air. She crooned over

Theodore, my aunt's old teddy bear, while smoothing his worn fur, fogging his golden eyes with her sherry-soaked breath. Hesitant to interrupt, my sister, brother and I stood in the doorway, waiting for the spring ritual to begin.

We helped Granny pull a trunk from under the basement stairs. Entombed inside were dozens of white tissue mummy bundles. Under Granny's watchful eye, we carefully unwrapped doll after doll. There was a Greek soldier in white skirts and red leather shoes; an Indian woman in a spangled sari; a spirited flamenco dancer; Scots in kilts; a Dutch boy and girl in wooden shoes; a shepherd; and a dark woman who wore beaded necklaces and carried a jar on her head. We marveled over the dolls, aired them in her fragrant garden, then carefully wrapped them up and put them away for another year. They were interesting but we did not love them nor cherish the ritual. With every trip she took, Granny added to this collection. These dolls were for my sister and me, but always for "later." When Granny died, however, the trunk full of dolls was gone, its whereabouts a mystery. Perhaps she knew we didn't share her need to have us love dolls. Perhaps she had given them to others less fortunate.

I was captured one day when I was four, taken to Children's Orthopedic Hospital, imprisoned in a bed with high sides and left alone. I screamed for hours. No one answered my night bell so I had to pee in my bed. Something was wrong with my legs, but it still took three adults to hold me down while a fourth stabbed my butt with a needle every day for two weeks. I learned that I was lucky. Some kids with polio had legs like toothpicks.

After I was released and our quarantine ended, my uncle gave me a clown doll with a hard plastic face. Clownie's cheeks were soon permanently dented and his white satin suit smeared with wet green paint from the bridge railings where I leaned to watch swirling whirlpools at Deception Pass.

My boyfriend Johnny and I were inseparable. That fall we entered kindergarten where he learned that boys should not like girls and abruptly stopped playing with me. But I still had Clownie. When we were alone, Clownie became the Little Boy who walked along minding his own business. He would fall in the street and the Big Nurse would rush out to help him, take him inside and make him her captive. She loved him but he only wanted to escape. She would beat him to try to make him love her, then cry for forgiveness. This game was very hard on Clownie. One night I was devastated to see Clownie's head poking out of the garbage can. Wailing, I snatched him out, starting a tug-of-war with my mother. What she saw as a ruined plaything was in truth the object of my passion, my beloved. But she won the ensuing battle and Clownie found his freedom in the great landfill in the sky.

There were other brushes with dolls. For instance, one summer our family spent a week with Auntie Nell who lived by a pristine Canadian lake. Its clear water suspended us between the ethereal sky and a lake bed strewn with drowned trees.

Auntie Nell's Scottish brogue was so thick we children could barely understand her when she fixed us with the stake of her gaze, deeply sunken eyes glittering, thin lips peeled back from her yellow teeth in a skeletal grin that turned our minds to jello.

My brother, sister and I spent the week on her rickety dock. Barb worked on her tan while my brother Skip waged wars with his toy soldiers. I swam deep under water searching for treasure. Beneath the dock I found a jar full of dark water and soft, bobbing objects. Probing confirmed my suspicions – turtle eggs. I felt the hard fetal turtle inside one. My parents' suggestion that someone had knocked a jar of olives off the dock did not amuse me.

Another dive took me deep among the branches and muck of the lake bottom. My hand closed around something like a baseball just as I pushed off for the surface, heart pounding as the bony branches scrabbled at my legs. Plumes of dark mud streamed from the object in my hand. As I neared the surface it became faintly recognizable – a shrunken head! I erupted from the water with a gurgling scream and flung it away. It landed on the dock, splattering my brother and sister as I scrambled up the ladder. We clutched each other in horror. The empty eye sockets of the shrunken head transfixed us as mud slid down the face to reveal pink plastic doll lips parted in a faint grin.

The head freed us from our stupefaction around Auntie Nell, and it came home to rest in my curio drawer beside the jar of turtle eggs. Years later while reminiscing over the treasures in that drawer, I learned about transmutation, whereby a thing changes into something else. Close examination of the turtle eggs revealed that they had mysteriously become olives. I don't know what became of the head.

My adult life filled with work, travel, lots of interesting and challenging things, but a sweet and genuine love eluded me, spooked by fear of loss and capture, I suppose. A few years ago an idea began calling for attention, taking root: I was to create an ancestor figure. "Me? Make a doll? No way, I don't do dolls!"

But the idea from someplace deep would not leave me alone, intruding even on my dreams. Eventually I gave in and began tentatively, fumbling not only with the materials but with having to nurture this being, with learning to listen to her. She shaped me while I shaped her. Giving her a body of soft brown leather felt right. I learned that she had purple iridescent beaded hair and that she chose to fit easily in my hand. I learned that being female was a good thing. Soon after, I met the love my life, now my husband.

Once proud that I did not play with dolls, I later found them to be a necessary learning experience. Very powerful, this playing with dolls – not for sissies.

~

Kari (rhymes with starry) Berger: "Loving animals and making things are passions which have defined me since the beginning. I relish being in my cozy workroom surrounded by piles of luscious stuff, like beads, fabrics, paints, boxes and some dolls I've made. Along with my ancestor doll, there's Salina, the belly dancer and her lover Billy Bones made for my wonderful husband Gary, who wanted a doll.

I'm currently working in photography and researching my grandfather's Alaska Gold Rush experiences. I find not a day goes by without a gift of remarkable light, often in the most mundane of circumstances."

I met Kari at a cloth doll convention in San Francisco, California, where we discovered we wouldn't have had to travel so far to meet. In our hometown, Seattle, we not only had dollmaking studios in the same building but they were just three doors away from one another on the same floor. During the several years since then, we've discovered many mutual interests besides dolls.

Photos: Kari with Clownie, Grandpa Hazeltine and sister Barbara Berger. Knute E. Berger, Photographer. Kari's ancestor doll. Kari Berger, photographer.

Dianne Hicks Morrow

Christmas Eve

Christmas Eve

Eight-year-old doubting Thomasina,
I ask my mother, "How will Santa find me
on the train?" Miles and miles of
Christmasy trees speed by the window
as she covers me up and explains,
"He knows where you are, you'll see."
I still want to believe.
Visions of my dream dolly
dance through my head, then fade.
How will he even get on this train
and will he know I'm the girl who
wants the large-as-life doll?
I drift in and out of fitful sleep,

want to be awake to tell him
I'd be in my own bed at home 'cept we're going
to Montreal for Christmas with my cousins.
No sign of Santa – where is he? Is he?
One eye opens to daylight and motion.
Where am I? Mom and Dad asleep across from me
baby asleep beside me – what baby?
"He came, he came!" I yell. He is, he is.
 Mom and Dad are happy to tell me,
"Santa got on the train in Sherbrooke, Quebec."
I believe, I believe, I believe he did.
Here is Chuckles, so life-like
the conductor has to do a recount,
one extra head on this train
since crossing the border. A stowaway?
I'm thrilled when he asks if this is
my baby sister or a doll. Relieved,
he laughs at his mistake.
Chuckles' big blue eyes open and close,
real lashes, not painted on,

her body soft in her hand-knitted dress.
Dimpled elbows and knees, flushed baby cheeks.
Only the raised rubber curls give her away,
if you look closely under her knitted bonnet.
My Santa-on-the-train story leaves my
doubting older cousins speechless.
Back home one winter night
Mom and Dad have friends in for bridge.
Awake in bed I overhear them talk.
"How did we get that big doll on the train?
I'll tell you it wasn't easy," laughs Mom,
"It took up most of the space in one suitcase!"
In the dark I blush, don't let on
I hear, even to myself.

~

Dianne Hicks Morrow stays connected to her childhood in as many ways as possible. An award-winning poet, whose poems featuring childhood memories have appeared in several Canadian literary journals, she is completing her first poetry manuscript. Having lived on Prince Edward Island for over twenty-five years, she continues her childhood search for kindred spirits, first inspired by Lucy Maud Montgomery's Anne of Green Gables. Her dream is to complete a best-seller based on interviews she is doing with people of all ages about their quests for kindred spirits.

I met Dianne while visiting a friend on Prince Edward Island. After we wrote together one evening, Dianne told me this story about Chuckles.

Photo: Dianne with Chuckles and the sleigh Dianne's father made for Chuckles.

Jeanne M. Barrett

The Girls and I

The Girls and I

I was an only child for six years. During that time, I lived much in my mind, peopling my days with what adults called "imaginary friends." My sense of who I was and who I could become was communicated tenderly with my dolls. I was blessed with a mother and a maternal grandmother who allowed me a full range of fantasy and assisted me in the details.

Besides my friend Julie, who was invisible to all but me, and my beloved pets, my dearest friends were four dolls. Each doll was finely crafted with rooted hair, eyelashes, eyes that opened and closed, and movable leg and arm joints. Each expressed – and continues to express – a different aspect of my identity. Each possessed a wardrobe of beautifully-made clothes, contributed by my grandmother, crafted from scraps of clothing made for me and my mother.

Poor Pitiful Pearl was an oval-faced ragged child who arrived in orphan clothes and without shoes. Her face was sad and wistful in expression. She contained all my loneliness and heartbreak. I could – and still can – weep with her.

Marybell Get Well came equipped with crutches, casts, spots to simulate chicken pox and measles and hospital-appropriate garb. She had a hopeful and sweet expression, and a round, healthy form. With her, I could be ill myself, or I could nurture her through sickness as I wanted to be nurtured. And she could always get well!!

Alyce was the doll of my ultimate fantasy. She was a ballerina, with toe shoes and rhinestone earrings for the spotlight. She was as elegant and graceful and lovely as I ever wanted to be, and she received the applause and acknowledgment for her skill and beauty and grace that seemed so completely inaccessible to me. With her, I was the adored center, the shimmering talented one, the star.

My Shirley Temple doll spanned time most of all, for she was a real person, who had grown up and was telling stories on TV. Although she came to me dressed as a shepherd girl with dimples and curls, I knew she had a future. Her smile showed teeth and would become an adult smile, speaking to me. She gave me a strong sense of growing out of my quiet loneliness. The world had only to discover me, and I could tell stories too!

It is painful and wonderful for me to embrace these dolls now. I relive my longing and my faith. I am sad, recovering, graceful, a storyteller, the center of much attention, and a child alone.

~

Jeanne hails from the planet Mongo, and has incarnated in Seattle to learn humor and grace. She seeks active stillness by teaching the Alexander Technique. She also collects pebbles and stones.

I met Jeanne when I was looking for a teacher of the Alexander Technique in my quest for relief from carpal tunnel syndrome. I had read of a man's recovery from this condition after practicing the Alexander Technique.

Photo: Jeanne took this photo of her girls.

Laura Strance Poston
Sarah Poston Bartos

Sarah Jane

Sarah Jane

Laura: The two beautifully dressed, fragile dolls were arranged sitting up against the pillows on the elegant bed in the guest room. Aunt Laura was excited as she led me, Laura Jane, her namesake, and my mother into the room. Our family was visiting from Seattle and had traveled to Dallas by train. This trip was an amazing adventure in my three year-old life. Aunt Laura anticipated I would excitedly reach for the dolls she had waiting for me. Instead, I stood paralyzed, staring at them, feeling they were too beautiful, too precious for me to touch, much less play with! I politely acknowledged the presentation of the dolls and quickly escaped to the safety of the kitchen with Vassar, the cook. There, the simplicity of life was more like home than the palatial elegance of the rest of the southern mansion.

So began my life with dolls. It did not take many years for me to establish myself as a tomboy, playing dramatic games of make-believe in the woods with my friends and in the pasture with the horses. I was not a "doll person." They were toys to be played with but not real live people or playmates.

As I grew older, the dolls from Texas stayed in the attic in the cradle that had been my mother's when she was a child. When mother was ready to sell the house, I was asked to take the things I wanted to keep. There was no question that the dolls and cradle should move to our house. My two year-old daughter Sarah was showing a propensity toward dolls. I thought when she was older, Sarah might like having a cradle that had been her grandmother's and dolls that had been owned – though spurned – by her mother. So the Texas dolls came to Dobbs Ferry, New York. And where did they go? To the attic, of course!

Sarah: When I was a little girl I was convinced I had been born a century too late and in the wrong part of the country. I would sit up late on warm summer nights looking at the stars and imagine what life had been like one hundred years before. How I longed to be a pioneer girl on the wild western frontier.

We lived far from the West in an old house with a creaky attic which I would investigate alone. I knew every piece of furniture and the contents of every box. I kept my special treasures in the old rolltop desk with the secret drawer. When I opened the lid of my mother's cedar chest, a rich cedar smell rose to greet me. My eyes took in the finely-pressed linens and special lace tablecloths given to my mother by my grandmother.

I pictured my grandmother, who was so refined, setting out fresh blackberry cobbler on fine china plates elegantly arranged on the fine linens.

One day when I was looking through the cedar chest, I came across my mother's dolls from her childhood that had been given to her by her rich aunt from Texas. The strings that had held their heads and limbs tight were sagging, but they still looked life-like. There was a baby doll, a pretty blond doll and Sarah Jane. I loved her right away and I knew Sarah Jane would be her name because of a doll I had met through a book called *Amy's Doll*. It is the story of a little girl named Amy who longs for an old-fashioned doll she sees in the window of a store and she gets it for her birthday. Amy names her doll Sarah Jane and they have a very special friendship. Amy brings her to dinner, takes her to tea parties and even lets her touch her rock collection. One day Sarah Jane gets left out in the snow and is ruined, so Amy and her mother take her to a doll hospital where a nice man repairs her. It was my favorite book and I asked to hear it again and again. I had the book memorized before I could read. I still know the story by heart.

I knew the doll was a link between my mom and me. Mom's middle name is Jane and my name is Sarah, so it all felt very magical to me. When I lifted that old doll from among the linens, I knew she was Sarah Jane and that *Amy's Doll* had entered my real life.

Sarah Jane became my playmate. She was like a real little girl – practical and down-to-earth – someone with whom I could really be friends. My mother told me that her hair was real. It smelled old and felt brittle. I wondered whose hair it had been and why she had cut it off. Was she poor or just tired of the long burden? I thought I'd clean it up a bit and gave her a trim, but somehow as I went along, her bangs got pretty short. Much to my sorrow, they wouldn't grow back. But it was just hair. Playing was the most important thing and we had a lot of playing to do.

Laura: Sarah cared for her doll the best way she could, although like her mother before her, she was not a gentle companion. One day when Sarah was eleven years old the thirty-five year-old elastics that held Sarah Jane together gave out and the doll fell apart. She put Sarah Jane's pieces into a bag and inquired, with an enlightened reader's mind, about a doll hospital. Searching through the Yellow Pages, I discovered that every doll hospital in Westchester County had gone out of business. My schedule was already busy, so I just let the problem rest since Sarah was not in her peak doll years, or so I thought. What a surprise to discover that Sarah's great wish for her twelfth birthday was to find a doll hospital to fix Sarah Jane. That propelled me into action. I looked through the New York City Yellow Pages and found that the New York Doll Hospital on Lexington Avenue was not only still in business but open on Saturdays.

Thus a plan developed. We would buy tickets for the musical *Fiddler on the Roof.* Sarah was in a school performance and knew all the lyrics and music. We would go to the doll hospital first, then to lunch and the musical. If all went well, we might even pick up the doll after the performance.

On the appointed day, we were up early for the drive into Manhattan. Luck was with us. We located the doll hospital and even found metered parking for thirty minutes nearby. Sarah clutched the bag with the pieces of Sarah Jane in her arms. We walked up the steps into a most amazing shop full of dolls, parts for dolls and all kinds of old-fashioned doll accessories. It was very quiet and we wondered if anyone was there. Finally a nice man came out and Sarah and I together explained what we wanted. As we were talking, I kept having a strange feeling about the man and his shop. I felt that somehow I knew the man, that I had seen him before – somewhere.

Sarah: I'll never forget the experience of walking into that doll hospital. Mom and I recognized the assorted piles of doll heads and limbs as being like those pictured in *Amy's Doll*. We stood awe struck, for the man who greeted us from behind the counter was the man pictured in the photos in the book. It was a magical moment. Just as Amy's doll had entered my life, I had entered the doll hospital of my favorite book and Sarah Jane would be repaired by the same kindly man who had restored Amy's Sarah Jane.

Laura: Soon the story came spilling out – Sarah's love for the book, her memorizing it, Sarah's doll being named for the doll in the book and the man's resemblance. Shyly,

the man told us this was the shop that had been photographed for the book and he was the man pictured in the story. We talked and talked until I remembered thirty minutes on the parking meter. What an amazing and wonderful set of circumstances this was to celebrate a special birthday.

The rest of the day was wonderful but for me it was all anticlimactic. Every once in awhile I had to pinch myself to believe these amazing coincidences had happened. After *Fiddler,* which was splendid, we drove back to the doll hospital and picked up Sarah Jane, who was ready and waiting. What a reunion. She was whole again. I realized for the first time that just as Sarah loved this doll, so did I! She was something that we shared and both of us, in different ways, were delighted to have her back in the family, intact.

Sarah: Sarah Jane lives in my mother's attic near Seattle. Sometimes I still miss her and I think about calling mom and asking her to send her to me. But I have no place for her now and she is better off among her friends of antiquity in the attic. She is a doll of the past but also the future because you can bet as soon as I have a little girl, if I am so honored, I'll be reading her *Amy's Doll* and calling Mom and asking for Sarah Jane.

What magic will she see or was it just me?!

~

Laura Strance Poston is a native of western Washington, a third-generation descendant of early settlers to the Puget Sound region. As a teacher and non-profit school administrator, she has worked in public and independent schools in New York, Washington and Pennsylvania. Laura and her husband of forty-two years, Thurman, raised their two children in Dobbs Ferry, New York. They are now back in the Puget Sound region, short flights from their children in California and Colorado.

My friend Jeanne Barrett introduced me to Laura.

Sarah Poston Bartos was raised in the Hudson River Valley of New York. Her love of the pioneer lifestyle and natural environment expanded as she moved from New York to New Hampshire, Oregon, Washington and Colorado. As a nurse, she specialized in homecare and care of the elderly for fourteen years. She is studying to become a nurse practitioner. She lives in Boulder, Colorado, with her husband David and their year-old son, Mikhal Jan. She still enjoys communing with nature in the Rocky Mountains.

I became acquainted with Sarah by telephone.

Photos: Sarah Jane with *Amy's Doll* (by Barbara Brenner, photos by Sy Katzoff, 1963)
Kari Berger, photographer.
Laura Jane, age eight.
Young Sarah and Snoopy.

Soosi Watts Day

Rose Mary Gets Rescued

Rose Mary Gets Rescued

I was barely two years old on the morning I toddled down the narrow stairs from "the star room" to the sound of early morning music. A mysterious glow from the brightly-lit tree cast magical shadows on the stairwell to my bedroom. Below, in the darkness, the greens and reds of the Christmas tree lights gave a sneak preview of packages of all sizes and shapes.

At the center of this magic was a shiny, round, red child-size table with black metal legs and two matching red chairs. Seated across from one another was an unlikely pair – Rose Mary, a solemn-faced cloth doll with a pinafore over her tiny-checked, blue gingham dress and a dust cap covering her hairless head and Uncle Marvin, a jubilant, grinning clown wearing a tall pointed cap of striped pillow-ticking perched precariously on a froth of red yarn hair.

I have been told that I stood and stared for the longest time, then slowly descended the remaining stairs and walked wordlessly to the table, picked up the clown, looked at Rose Mary and wistfully said, "Poor Soosi, no cups!" My memory of that day is limited to the extraordinary sense of magic that I felt, the arrival of two lifetime companions, and my sense of having tremendous responsibility for the well-being of these kindred spirits.

Rose Mary and Uncle Marvin became my constant companions who knew no danger. They hung from our balcony over the rising Puget Sound waters. They rode in my little red bucket to the beach below. Rose Mary even took my place on the dreaded wooden doughnut of the toitee with the duck in front. They were dragged from one beach find to another, their clothes filling with bits of crushed shell and sand fleas - that is, on the days they wore clothes!

On one most unfortunate day, Rose Mary fell from her lookout position on the balcony into the deep salt waters below. It was high tide. Her cotton body quickly absorbed the cool brine, making her heavy and driftily drawing her to the pebbled sea floor. From above, I could see her solemn, unsmiling face looking up from the bottom while little rock crabs probed her limp and pasty-white arms and legs.

"The cwabs are eating Wose Mawey! The cwabs are eating Wose Mawey!" I shrieked at the top of my nearly three-year-old lungs. There was no consoling this frenzied doll-mother until Daddy trolled up and down in our old wooden boat, dragging a large fishnet alongside.

"Poor Wose Mawey, poor Wose Mawey!" I crooned from the balcony edge.

On the third swoop of the net, Rose Mary arose from the depths, dripping and staring straight ahead. Her limp, soggy limbs were akimbo in the net. Daddy was jubilant.

White Knight to the rescue. He would get mileage out of this rescue for years to come and remained my white knight until his untimely death eighteen years later.

My calm and ever-so-dutiful mother rushed Rose Mary to her makeshift doll hospital. She hung her with wooden clothespins to a wire strung in the kitchen over the narrow trash burner. Though her expression didn't change, Rose Mary looked sad and alone dangling over the burner. A slow, rhythmic progression of salty droplets fell from her bare cotton feet onto the wood stove, bouncing and popping, then disappearing mysteriously.

That night, instead of the usual story from a book, we talked about what Rose Mary and Uncle Marvin might be doing in the kitchen while I slept. I was certain Uncle Marvin was doing somersaults for Rose Mary to cheer her up. Mama said she was going to wash and iron Rose Mary's dress, pinafore and pantaloons so they would be ready for her once she was dry. And yes, she would undoubtedly be dry by morning. I fell asleep watching glow-in-the-dark decals of the Runaway Dish and the Spoon on my chest of drawers fade out of sight in the darkness.

In the morning, I was first to stir. I climbed out of bed and slipped down the stairs in my pajamas-with-feet. I raced to the kitchen to see if Rose Mary was dry. She was gone! Two large wooden clothes pins remained where Rose Mary had been attached to the wire. The trash burner was cold. There was no sign of her. I felt scared and my tummy churned. I began to cry.

I padded into the tiny living room and there, under the stairwell, was the little red table and chairs. In one chair sat Uncle Marvin. In the other chair, looking as good as her first morning under the tree, sat Rose Mary, with the familiar solemn expression painted on her face. Her gingham dress was freshly ironed, her dust cap and pinafore starched. In front of each, on tiny china plates, were little tea cakes. Peppermint honey-water tea waited in the teapot and at last there were tea cups for the three of us to enjoy tea. A special twinkle shone in the black button eyes of Uncle Marvin and his red hair was mussed. A crudely-penciled note sat on the table:

> Soosi
>
> THANK YOU FOR RESCUING ME FROM THE CRABS. THEY SURELY WOULD HAVE TAKEN MY FINE DUST CAP AND WOULD HAVE UNRAVELED MY SEAMS IF YOU HAD NOT CALLED FOR HELP. I DON'T THINK I SHOULD LIKE TO SIT ON THE BALCONY LEDGE AGAIN ANY TIME SOON.
>
> Rosemary

Rose Mary never went near water again.

~

Soosi Watts Day was born and raised in Olympia, Washington, where she had the shores of Puget Sound and the rural fields and bogs of farm land to wander as a child. She and her husband Ed live near Olympia. Soosi is an elementary school counselor.

I met Soosi when she was dating my brother during our college days. We reconnected decades later when Soosi learned I was living a short distance away and looked me up.

Photo: Soosi's studio portrait at age three.

Grace Leaf Bartels

Gifts

Gifts

She had deep auburn hair that cascaded past her waist. Her skin was silky smooth and creamy. Her dress of green and gold buttoned up the back. She wore a smile that said that she would be a devoted friend. This doll's name was Crissy. On a bitterly cold winter morning in Seoul, Crissy was placed in my arms by the man and woman I was to call Dad and Mom. I had never before seen hair the color of fire. I fixed my eyes on Crissy, who would be the first of many gifts to come. This kind couple spoke a different language, but not really. They knew that all little girls needed a friend to share their innermost secrets with, especially a little girl who was about to leave behind everything she knew to start a better life.

Crissy guarded me through the long nights while I lay in bed, alone in the darkness, crying out for my Oma. I knew Oma loved me very much and had selflessly given me up to this couple to take good care of me and give me an education in a way Oma could not. Still, I missed sleeping beside my mother, breathing in concert with the woman who had protected and nurtured me and, in the end, had fled – penniless and frightened – from the tormented husband and father who yelled and screamed and threw things when he drank. No matter where my mother and I had slept – such as the frigid floor of a storage closet – at least we had been together. Now my tummy was full for the first time, and I was warm and safe in my own room, in a house with heat – things I had longed for – but I was so alone. I was afraid to go to sleep, for sleep was what I had succumbed to that night my mother left me with this couple. Upon awakening, I found myself thrust into these peoples' lives and they in mine. Although Crissy sat just inches away from my tear-streaked face, I would not be consoled by my doll's nightly vigil.

It was long after the bitter winds of Pusan abated, the snows drifted and melted away and the flowers bloomed again, that I finally stopped screaming in the night for Oma and began singing with Crissy at my bedside. Now I couldn't even remember my futile pleas for my mother in Korean. Ditties sprang from me in flawless English. Images of my mother came to me only in dreams. My mother would sob and speak in English, telling me to be a good girl, an obedient daughter, but I could never respond. I was rendered speechless in my sleep, paralyzed and unable to touch the phantom figure floating before me.

In America, I played jump rope with girls who had big blue eyes and hair the color of straw. Some even had strands of fire shooting from their heads like Crissy. No one I knew liked kimpop, nor could anyone fathom eating such a strange creation – rice with seaweed? And one friend who spent the night balked during dinner because she wanted milk and sugar on her rice, not "plain and yucky!"

My seventh birthday party had come and gone in the summer, so I was confused when another party was thrown six months later. Hailed as Crissy's "birthday," December 1 was the day I had been given to my new Mom and Dad a year earlier. For her birthday dinner, Crissy and I ate teriyaki chicken and rice and kimchi. After dinner, there were gifts to open. Every year after that, Crissy's birthday was celebrated in the same fashion, in honor of the love that a little girl can find from the kindest of strangers and of the strength even little girls can muster in the face of all things that are so terrible and terrific at the same time. Crissy turns twenty-four this year. (1997)

~

Grace Leaf Bartels began life as Kim Seung Min. When her mother made the ultimate sacrifice of giving her up for adoption so she could receive an education and have a better life, Grace became the beloved daughter of Lawrence and Faith Leaf. She was raised deep in a hundred-acre wood in Addy, Washington, near Spokane, with an adopted sister named Anne, coyotes, skunks and bears, and – oh, yes – a doll named Crissy. Grace is a counselor at Spokane Community College and is working on her Ph.D. She lives with her husband Rick and five year-old son Ben.

I met Grace in my living room when she and Rick, newly engaged, came to visit my son, Brad. Rick and Brad were the dearest of friends since high school. After Rick and Grace married, they traveled to Korea, where Grace was reunited with her birth mother.

Photo: Grace and Crissy.

Tony Hattell

King of Toys

King of Toys

When Christmas or birthdays came round, we always got everything we ever wanted. My parents were too generous. As a result, we were a little spoiled. I grew up in the seventies with all sorts of great toys to choose from: Hot Wheels, Matchbox cars, Vertibird Star Trek figures and Micronauts. But the best toy, the king of all toys, was G. I. Joe.

G. I. Joe first came out in 1964, two years before I was born. At first, Hasbro made Joe as a strictly military doll. He could be a soldier, sailor, marine or pilot. They even gave Joe some opponents like the German storm trooper or the Imperial Japanese soldier. What made Joe so great was the equipment. His uniforms were very detailed, with chevrons on the arms indicating rank, brass buttons for the dress uniforms and an Order of Lenin medal for the Russian soldier. The weapons were authentic as were the ammo boxes, TNT wire, sleeping bags, and tents. You name it, Joe had it. During the Vietnam War, however, Hasbro shifted G. I. Joe from a soldier to an adventurer and that's when I began getting the dolls.

My first Joe was a talker with fuzzy hair. You pulled a string on his chest and he said, "Cover me. I'll get the machine gun!" or "Take the Jeep and get some ammo- FAST!" Printed right on the box was a warning that said "Do not immerse in water," so naturally that was the first thing I did. I was only five!

The best thing about having a Joe was that now I could play with the big kids in our neighborhood. My brother, Curt, was five years older and, until I had a Joe of my own, I wasn't very welcome to join his playtime with his friends. I could watch, but I could not touch any of his things, probably because I would go into his room when he wasn't around and play with his toys and usually break something. My brother was a true G. I. Joe genius. Our backyard was transformed into a giant playland. Curt would run a hose through Mom's flower bed and turn it into a swamp on Guadalcanal. The shrubs were nests for snipers. He would camouflage them so well, sometimes the snipers were left there forgotten. He dug a trench that would fit a platoon of Joes complete with sandbags and machine guns and mortar pits. Curt was defending our backyard from Nazi or Communist hordes or whatever enemy made him mad that day.

The real fun of G. I. Joe was dressing him, putting on his equipment and posing him. It was important to me that Joe always be comfortable and warm and I never left him lying around without any clothes on. After all the effort of dressing and equipping him, some kids would heave rocks at their Joes to simulate a battle. We did not mistreat our Joes in this way. Curt made me think of Joe as my best friend and who wants to throw rocks at a best friend?

Since the military Joe had been retired, I could only buy Adventure Team Joes from the shelves at Sears or their Christmas Wishbook. Adventure Team Joe was more concerned with searching for stolen idols, capturing rare tigers for zoos and fighting off giant squids. This was fine unless you had a brother who grew up with the army Joes and was trying desperately to mold you in his image. We found a store in Spokane that still had all of the old Joe dolls and paraphernalia for a discount price. It was perfect for us because they were practically giving guns and uniforms away. I'll never forget getting a Russian uniform set and Curt helping me put it all together for display. He said, "If you keep him on the shelf like this, you'll never lose any parts." Curt always took good care of his toys and I didn't. His things were always clean and complete. I used every ounce of willpower I possessed to stop myself from taking that Russian Joe apart, but to no avail. Within five minutes, I had broken the gun and lost two grenades.

As time passed and Curt put away childish things, he gave me his mother lode of Joes and equipment including his first old Joe with painted hair from the sixties. I felt a kind of sadness and I promised to take care of these special things as if they really didn't belong to me. But playtime is rough and most of the Joes ended up broken or buried in the dirt pile. One day some of my friends and I were playing and I broke Curt's original Joe. I felt terrible but knew I'd feel even worse if he found out. I tried hiding it, even lied to keep the truth from him, but it didn't work. He was mad and I felt I had betrayed him. He looked at the broken Joe and said "Nice goin'," then walked away. That's when I stopped playing with Joes. Mom packed away whatever remained and soon I no longer needed childish things.

A couple years ago I was at Mom and Dad's house and feeling a little daffy. I went to the basement and found all the old Joes. They were all missing hands or heads or legs. I salvaged all the best uniforms and boots and rebuilt one complete Joe. I stuck the old painted head on the body, dressed him up and put him on a shelf at my home. He'll never go through the rigors of the backyard dirt pile, but sometimes when I walk by the shelf and no one's looking, Joe and I battle Nazis or Communists or whoever I'm mad at that day.

$\sim$

Tony grew up in the farming community of Pomeroy, Washington. He is a teacher and antiques buff. Old toys are among his varied collections. He and his wife Michelle live in Spokane, Washington.

I met Tony because he and my son Brad were good friends for many years.

Photo: The G.I. Joe reassembled by Tony. Ryan Burns, photographer.

Margaret Walker

Learning From a Doll

Learning From a Doll

First grade introduced me to the magic of writing. Wide-eyed in my front-row seat, I watched as my teacher, Mrs. Geroy, drew circles and straight vertical lines on the blackboard. The magic words that went with this activity were, "If you can draw lines and circles, you can write!" Amazing! School was getting really interesting.

My parents were well-educated people. My mother had put herself through college during the Depression. My father was a self-educated intellectual who had quite happily recited Kipling from atop a kitchen stool at the age of five. They both read incessantly. It never occurred to either of them that I might be missing some basic knowledge that should have just rubbed off in our family.

They were quite shocked, I'm sure, to get a message from Mrs. Geroy sometime around Halloween. "Your daughter needs some help," it said. "She doesn't know her address, her phone number, or even how to count to ten! Do something!"

The first I knew of all this was a phone call in early December. My parents were out. As I shyly answered the phone in my very-little girl voice, the disembodied grown-up on the other end of the line asked for Mr. or Mrs. Bothwell. With the weight of the black receiver heavy in my hand, I breathed into the phone, "They're not here."

"Please give them a message. Tell them that the doll they ordered for Christmas has been finished. The recorded voice in it says, "My name is Margie Bothwell. I live at 3139 North Ridgeview Drive, Altadena, California. My telephone number is Sycamore 7-4904. Mrs. Geroy has taught me to count: one, two, three, four, five, six, seven, eight, nine, ten.""

"Okay. Bye."

Hmmm. Somebody was making a doll for my parents with a voice in it. It was obviously for me, since my name was Margie Bothwell and Mrs.Geroy was my teacher. I wondered why the grown-up would tell me about it. I dutifully passed on the message to my parents and remember the stunned look on their faces. Why in God's name would the blasted woman leave a message like that with a CHILD right before Christmas?! They probably swore.

My parents were connected with most of the major toy manufacturers in the country, especially those in Los Angeles. My father sold advertising space in trade magazines, including *Playthings Magazine*, the major publication in the toy trade. My mother was later both his secretary and the West Coast editor of *Playthings*. They were good friends with a number of people in the industry.

Having gotten the word from Mrs. Geroy to "Do something!" my parents arranged with one of the toy manufacturers to make me a talking doll as a tutor. This creation involved implanting a miniature record player with a tiny custom-made record in the doll's chest. The recording giving my vital statistics was activated by pressing a button at the doll's heart. This was, after all, in the early 1950's. Kidnapping was still a major concern after the Lindbergh baby had been taken. School was a mile away and I sometimes walked home with other kids. I was about to learn about bikes. I should know how to phone home.

In spite of the leak about my Christmas surprise, the doll was presented to me on Christmas morning. "Margie" was quite magnificent. Unlike anything I had ever seen, she was as big as me. She was something of a rag doll with a plastic face. She had round blue eyes, long painted eyelashes and a nice smile. She was able to wear my clothes, but at the bottom of her round and floppy stuffed legs were black cloth shoes that were sewn on.

I was a fairly isolated kid at the time with few playmates and, except for my Dalmatian puppy, none were girls. Next to my dog, "Margie" became my best friend. I dragged her around the house like an oversized teddy bear. I danced with her and fantasized conversations, adventures and friendships. We colluded in romance and foul play. And any time I wanted to, I could push the button on the box in her chest, and she would give my vital statistics.

Though commonplace now, dolls who talked were uncommon in 1950. There were a few baby dolls saying only "Maaamaaa" when put down on their backs. I loved the idea of taking "Margie" to school for show-and-tell. I was allowed to haul her to school sometime in the next couple of months before a new elementary school opened near my house and I lost Mrs. Geroy as my teacher. Standing tall with my huge, unique doll companion in front of the room, I played the recording for my classmates and Mrs. Geroy. I can only imagine the amazement on her face as she witnessed the extent to which my parents had gone in order to bring me up to snuff.

Though I barely remember show-and-tell that day, I do recall sitting on the playground steps at Edison Elementary afterwards at recess. I can picture the gray metal swing set with the stiff canvas seats standing empty next to the chain link fence by the eucalyptus-lined street on the west side of the playground. There was gray sand under the swings that got into my shoes. The sand was kept in place by wooden railroad ties like the ones edging the playground steps where I was sitting. Some older kids standing not far from me, one boy in particular, were laughing but I was crying. "Margie's" voice box had fallen out of her chest onto the sand. Her record player was broken. She never spoke again.

Even after she lost her voice, she and my dog were my best friends. We carried on our adventures and fantasies. I hauled her around the house until I outgrew her and the clothes we used to share. The hole in her chest remained empty, like a box in the wall where electrical plugs or light switches go.

So here I sit forty-five years later, having raised my own boys (who didn't have dolls and had no problem memorizing the important things in life). I'm delighted once again by the magic – the magic of learning to write in first grade, of a life-sized doll, of a custom-made voice hidden in a stuffed chest, of a child's playful imagination and of a parents' gift. And the magic of memory which so easily recites in my head at odd, otherwise grown-up moments, "My name is Margie Bothwell. I live at 3139 North Ridgeview Drive, Altadena, California. My telephone number is Sycamore 7-4904. Mrs. Geroy has taught me to count: one, two, three, four, five, six, seven, eight, nine, ten." It worked. I never forgot.

~

Margaret Walker – "In spite of a shaky start in elementary school, learning and education have become my life's work. I teach in graduate school and do educational and philosophical consulting. I am earning my doctorate in human development, focusing on the stories that make our lives meaningful. I live in Manchester, Washington, where my best friends are still my family and my dog. I no longer play with dolls. I play with storying and remembering." A quote she keeps on her desk:

She kept asking if the stories were true.

I kept asking her if it mattered.

We finally gave up.

She was looking for a place to stand

and I wanted a place to fly.

—Brian Andreas of *The StoryPeople*

I met Margaret because her son Ian and my son Ryan have been friends since high school and our paths eventually merged at one of Ryan's jazz concerts.

Photo: A studio portrait of young Margaret.

Carolyn Michael

In the Nick of Time

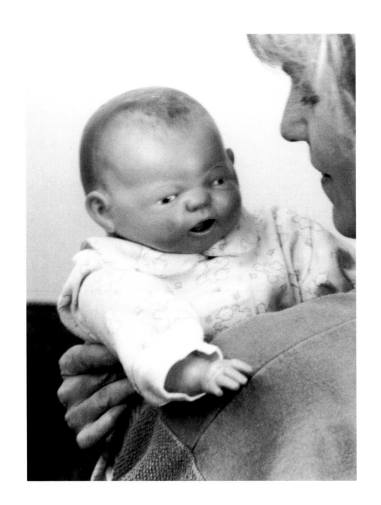

In the Nick of Time

I loved my baby doll even more than making mud pies or counting spots on lady bugs. She was the size of a real infant and felt as alive in my arms. She wore my old infant nightgowns, made and hand-embroidered with delicate flowers by my Mom. I named her Veronica after the black-haired beauty in the Archie comic books.

My little sister had a baby doll named Cathy who looked identical to mine in the eyes of everyone except us knowing doll mothers. Ginna and I played endlessly with our babies when we weren't fishing in the creek or picking alfalfa as pretend wheat harvests for our miniature farm by the chicken house. In the bare concrete basement of our home, we used cardboard boxes from Mom and Dad's hardware store to create walls, stoves, refrigerators – everything needed to make our own homes. Sometimes we'd visit "grandma" upstairs and our always busy mother would sit for a few minutes and rock our babies as she hummed a lullaby.

With Veronica and Cathy in tow, we moved from the farm when I was eight, bemoaning the fact our parents bought us a house in town rather than a horse. My older cousin, Diane, lived nearby and introduced me to the sophisticated world of paper dolls. We claimed a corner of their huge basement to create elaborate houses for our two-dimensional families. We were always making or looking for new furnishings and clothing. One day, having exhausted the resources in Aunt Agnes' Sears catalog, we raced to my house.

No one else was home. We headed straight to the basement to shop the endless stacks of old LIFE magazines. Veronica and Cathy were sleeping on the couch, just as Ginna and I had left them. Diane had never shown much interest in my baby doll world, but she seemed as concerned as I was to hear a distressing whimper coming from one of the babies. I was relieved to find my Veronica was fine but Cathy was definitely in pain. I poked gently into her soft abdomen and when I touched her lower right side, I immediately recognized the problem – an acute attack of appendicitis! My sister's appendix had been removed about a year earlier, so I not only recognized the symptoms, but knew the urgency of the situation. There was only one thing to do. Diane and I must perform an emergency appendectomy.

We quickly converted Dad's shop off the family room into an operating room. A sterile doll blanket was placed on the work table next to the vise and assorted screw drivers and pliers. We gathered the medical essentials – knife, scissors, needle and thread, tweezers. I rushed upstairs to grab bandages and Mercurochrome from the medicine cabinet. We scrubbed our hands and lovingly laid Cathy, naked but warm, on the surgical bed. We put a cloth with alcohol over Cathy's nose and mouth. It would have to do since we didn't have ether to anesthetize. I was the Doctor in charge. My able assistant handed me the knife. I carefully made a small slit in Cathy's flesh and finished it off with the scissors because they worked better. We were giddy with the excitement of examining Cathy's innards. We took turns with the tweezers, pushing aside little lumps of foam until at last we found and gently removed the inflamed culprit. Diane lit a match and sterilized the needle before we stitched up the incision. We liberally smeared Mercurochrome over and around the wound, its bright red glow further assuring us no infection would occur. We bandaged the incision so no dirt could get in, dressed Cathy in her nightie and put her back on the couch with a hug and a kiss.

When Mom and Ginna came home and learned of our heroic rescue, they were not properly impressed. Although Ginna was fleetingly annoyed, Mom was in such disbelief that we'd do such a thing that she wanted me to give Ginna my doll since we had ruined Cathy. Diane, being older, certainly should have known better! But we hadn't ruined Cathy. We had saved her. Mom must have realized that even a child mother cannot trade her baby for another because no adoptions took place. Veronica and Cathy eventually lived in a box in the attic as Ginna and I turned our interests towards boys and taping dried dance corsages to our dresser mirrors.

One day many years later at my parents' house, Mom and I were sharing our excitement over hearing from Ginna that she was expecting her first baby. But we lamented Ginna was living clear across the country in South Carolina. Mom came up with an idea. "Let's get Ginna's baby doll and send it to her. It can keep her company until the real baby arrives." We headed for the attic. Mom, knowing right where everything was, led us straight to the doll box. The excitement I felt opening that box was akin to poking around in

Cathy's innards those many years before. We laid aside my brother's raggedy old teddy bear, storybook dolls in stunning dresses and dolls with tattered hair and well-worn dresses. All were piled on top of our baby dolls resting at the bottom. I lifted the infants from their dark tomb. They were identical, all right, and at first glance I could no longer be sure which of the twins was mine. Mom and I started giggling as I peeked under the dolls' nighties. One had a sloppily stitched scar with faded remnants of Mercurochrome that had, indeed, kept Cathy from getting an infection.

"Now aren't you glad Diane and I performed that surgery?" I laughed.

Mom laughed too. "Yes, I'm glad we can send Ginna her own doll. But still, you and Diane should have known better!"

We wrapped Cathy in one of Ginna's baby blankets, laid her in the white wicker bassinet in which all three of us and my boys had slumbered and shipped them off to Ginna. She was delighted with the surprise. Several months later, Cathy gave up the bassinet to Nathan Meriwether Wise, Ginna's first real live baby.

~

Carolyn Michael – "I live in Olympia, Washington, near my sister, the waters of Puget Sound and several small farms. Veronica lives with me. Cathy's fate is uncertain. She disappeared somewhere in Arizona or El Salvador."

Photo: Carolyn holding Veronica. Kari Berger, photographer.

Heather Reedy

Bluebell Blouses

Bluebell Blouses

Rain. Rain and rain forests. Granite Falls. The Callahan's farm. Magical places to spend childhood weekends. Moss and ferns – tiny mushrooms and rocks – all miniature worlds where I imagined myself small and living, like the ladybug in one of my favorite childhood books. A flower would become a dress or a piece of furniture. Everything was lush and moist, powerfully green. Shades of green vividly return in my child's mind – sarsparilla soda green, deep forest greens. I wanted to live there on the moss rug under the baby ferns and pink flowers.

My friend Molly and I used to make tiny stick dolls with upside-down floral formals. Our dolls were only an inch or two high, and we'd hunt for clothes in neighboring yards. Bluebells were perfect for a hat or blouse, complimented by an azalea skirt or gown. If we were lucky we found berries for making their heads. We usually made several dolls because there were so many blossoms and it was easier than changing their clothes. Piercing flowers and keeping the ensemble together were somewhat delicate and precarious maneuvers. Then we'd float our creations on the lake that was a puddle in her back alley. We'd find bark or discarded cups and bits of paper for the sail, then blow or push our dressed sticks across the water, sometimes using long twigs to reach them without getting wet.

Entering these miniature worlds engrossed me for hours. But when it got too dark or we were hungry, Molly and I would drop everything and head inside. The boats and their passengers were left stranded in the middle of the lake, twigs resting at the bottom of the puddle. I wonder if anyone passing by our abandoned play site noticed the microcosm we had created, or if it just looked like bits of garbage with twigs and flowers floating aimlessly – in a puddle – in the alley.

~

Heather Reedy – "I live in Seattle with my husband Dan and our baby daughter Mim. I'm a Seattle native – born, raised and educated in Washington State. The story included here began as a five minute timed writing on "rain." The result is a memory I thought I'd lost but now embrace as I watch my daughter discovering her world. My lifelong enjoyment of creating spaces has translated into my art, my home and my home cleaning and organizing business. I see, I arrange and transform. I create."

I met Heather in Olympia where she and my son Brad were attending college. Brad introduced us when we bumped into her in an art gallery. When she left, I said, "SHE's nice." He ignored my intonation but months later he re-introduced her as his true love. She was his loving partner until his untimely death.

Photo: Heather during her stick and flower doll era. Mike Reedy, photographer.

Someko Kokita

All the Time Busy

by Carolyn Michael

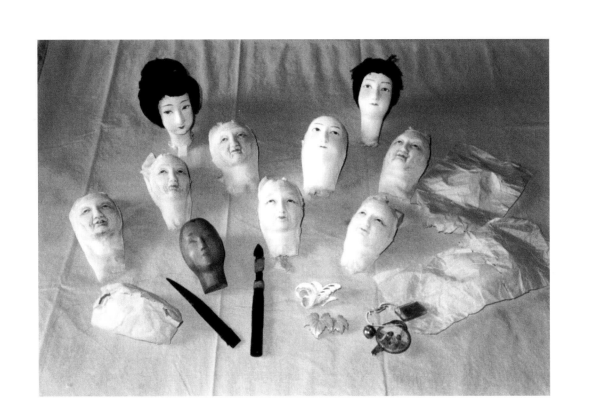

All the Time Busy

by Carolyn Michael

Someko "Some" (prounounced So-meh) Kokita greeted me at the door of her atrium with a grin as big as her almost four foot frame. It was her ninety-second birthday. Melissa Kokita had told me about her grandmother's fifty-year passion for making dolls and teaching the art to others. Melissa had graciously arranged not only for me to meet Some but for her mother, Rosie Kokita, to serve as interpreter.

"Hello. Hello. Come. Come." Some giggled with the delight of a child blowing bubbles and watching them float into the sky. She led me down the narrow hall that served as a personal museum reflecting a lifetime of creating simply for the joy of it. Every available space was filled with tiny, exquisite treasures made from old matchstick boxes to look like dressers; intricate architectural structures out of toothpicks and more Japanese dolls than a street of shops in Tokyo. I marveled not only at the volume and variety of her creations but the perfection shown in the completion of each one. As I repeatedly voiced my admiration, which Rosie reiterated in Japanese, Some would giggle and say "Busy, busy. All the time busy."

As I tried to take in the countless porcelain-faced dolls in their exquisite kimonos, I was captivated by a beautiful fabric-faced doll wearing a long, white tunic over her kimono, her arm around a child who clutched her one-inch doll. Another child was poised nearby holding her doll. The girls seemed to be waving a greeting.

"Tell me about these dolls," I asked. Some's eyes sparkled and with her now familiar grin, she said, "Made in internment camp." My heart struggled to match her words with her smile. My mind flooded with images and questions.

Rosie had fixed tea and muffins, so we went into the workroom where many of the creations had taken form. We sat on child-sized chairs at the work table as the story of the family's internment during World War II unfolded. Some was forty-two when her family was forced to leave their Seattle home and relocate to a camp for Japanese-Americans several miles south at Puyallup, Washington in 1942. Each person was allowed one suitcase and no cameras. They were later transferred to Camp Minidoka, Idaho, a barren desert where they would remain until the war ended three years later. Their family of six was given one room with a potbellied stove in the center. They had to stuff straw into cotton ticking to make their own mattresses, causing many people to suffer with asthma and hay fever.

Some's husband worked as a carpenter at the camp and availed himself of some wood scraps and built a partition in their solitary room, providing a luxury others didn't have. He made bunk beds and a piece of furniture that served as a davenport by day and a bed at night. The children went to school and the young adults were assigned various jobs. Mr. Kokita was kept busy doing carpentry but Some was bored with nothing to do. Before being taken to camp, she had done flower arranging, carved intricate jewelry of wood and abalone and performed the tea ceremony. A woman in camp was teaching doll making, so Some took her class. "I don't like, so… " she said with a giggle and a raised eyebrow, as she retrieved one of the woman's dolls to show Rosie and me.

So, she created her own dolls. Her husband made her two carving knives out of discarded pieces of metal and brought her scraps of wood to carve molds for her dolls' heads. I asked if she was looking at someone as a model when she carved them.

"No. Just thinking," she said. She saved rice from her dinner and mixed it with water until it was the right consistency to serve as glue. She carefully layered toilet paper and this glue over the mold until it was the proper thickness. For the final layer, she cut up their sheer curtains – her silk substitute – to give the face its wonderful texture. "Paste it down. Paste it down. Anything I use," she said, making the motions with her tiny, expressive hands. Some laid a carved mold on the table. A delicate, peaceful and perfectly symmetrical face stared up at me. "I have just one now," she said.

"How many molds did you make?" Rosie asked.

"I don't know. Soooo much. Busy, busy. All the time, busy," and Some went off to find some unfinished doll heads from those days at the camp.

She returned with eight painted faces, their papier-mache layers holding untold stories. There came a time during the internment when she was allowed to make small purchases. She chose to buy paints and cotton threads to sew on as hair, but she didn't have enough to buy brushes. "So what did you use to paint?" I asked.

"Toothpick," Some smiled as she held her fingers up to her mouth and made a rapid biting gesture.

"You just chewed it?" I exclaimed.

"So it makes…" and Some knew I could figure out the rest. I examined the intricate details in the dolls eyes and eyebrows, the wrinkles around the old women's eyes. I tried to imagine the movements of the toothpick paintbrushes in this creative woman's hands.

Others became interested in Some's dolls, so she started teaching classes. When her family was able to return to their home in 1945, Some continued to make dolls and teach doll-making. She abandoned her techniques of necessity and began making traditional Japanese dolls, ordering all manner of porcelain doll parts from Japan. Fifty years later, women were still gathering in her workroom every Wednesday afternoon. She was no longer actively teaching but providing an encouraging place for people to create and to have fun.

Having fun and enjoying life seem to be foremost on Some's agenda. As stories about her dolls spread, stores wanted to place orders but she refused. It would spoil the fun of it.

As I was preparing to leave, Some disappeared once again and this time returned – as you might have guessed – giggling. She was carrying the cloth dolls she kept on her bed. One was made by a student of hers and one she had made. But her favorite was the doll she had bought at the Puyallup Fair several years earlier. The grounds that once housed thousands of Japanese-Americans interned during the war now hosts the biggest fair in Washington State, attracting thousands for several days of fun and frolic. Her favorite doll, who has no name, has tears spilling down her face.

I began to ponder again the mystical power of dolls. I suspected this wonderful woman of wisdom would have some deep insights into this mystery, so I asked her, "Why do you think people all over the world love dolls? What is the fascination with dolls about?"

She looked at me with those smiling eyes and said, "I don't know!" She laughed an enormous laugh and this little woman who was all the time busy gave me a huge hug and bid me sayonara.

~

Someko "Some" Kokita was born in Tokyo in 1902. She came to live in America in 1923. She raised four children who gave her ten grandchildren. She passed away at her home at age ninety-six.

I met Some's granddaughter, Melissa Kokita, at a crafts class. She introduced me to her grandmother.

Photo:1) Carving knives, unfinished doll heads, and the mold used to make them.
2) Dolls Mrs. Kokita made while interned at Camp Minidoka. Kari Berger, photographer.
3) Mrs. Kokita at age 92 with her favorite dolls. Carolyn Michael, photographer.

Floyd Bell

Carving Culture

by Carolyn Michael

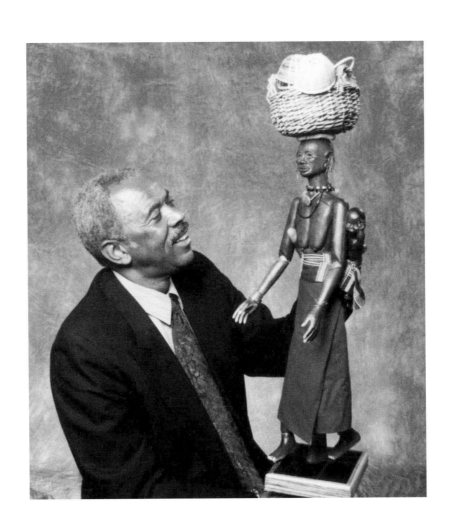

Carving Culture

Harriet Tubman. Booker T. Washington. Malcom X. Their likenesses and those of many historical figures have been carved out of black walnut by Floyd Bell's talented hands, guided by his caring heart. Inspired by their examples, Floyd creates tributes to great people who have made a difference in the lives of Americans today. Floyd says, "My dolls tell a story of people from Africa who were torn from their homeland and enslaved in foreign lands. I try to capture in the faces of my dolls the pain and suffering, the dignity and resolve, of a people who have endured."

Floyd teaches industrial arts at Westchester High School in Los Angeles, California, specializing in woodworking. He has followed his father's advice to "learn at least three ways to earn a living." His wife Sandra has had a passion for collecting dolls for many years. Her interest, as well Floyd's own students, got him started creating figures out of wood. One day in 1979, Floyd was encouraging his students, many of whom are underprivileged inner-city youth, to use their imaginations and the skills they'd learned to make something of value out of wood. Perhaps it was the doubtful looks that gave Floyd the impulse to pick up a scrap of wood and say, "Take this scrap of wood, for example. I can make a doll out of this wood and sell it." He began sculpting as someone muttered, "Yeah, right, Mr. Bell."

Over the next couple months, the students watched as Floyd transformed the wood scrap into a fully-jointed doll. She became a classroom playmate. Her limbs were broken and glued back together several times. Floyd took his willowy, peg-legged lady around town and was offered $75 for her. He kept the doll, which he had carved for his wife, proving his claim to her that he could design dolls of finer quality than the ones she was collecting at that time. And he not only made his point to his students, he soon had them busily creating their own doll figures. A rugged football player could be seen walking the halls with his doll tucked under his arm.

Using dollmaking as an enticement, Floyd has stimulated a new interest for his students. In 1994, with the assistance of his family and a few colleagues, he founded the Floyd Bell Scholarship Foundation to assist financially disadvantaged graduates who yearn for a college education. The Foundation has helped many deserving young people achieve their educational goals.

As a self-taught artisan, Floyd continued to make dolls. He entered them in competitions and won many awards, making Belle Dolls famous around the world. Floyd's dolls can be found in the Louvre Museum in Paris, the Wanke Doll Museum in Germany and many private collections. In 1991 he was chosen as a doll artist member of the prestigious National Institute of American Doll Artists (NIADA). Floyd was one of the artists selected to make an historical doll for a special White House Christmas tree in 1999. His mother, Modie Bell once remarked, "Child, I never would have thought that people would make so much fuss about dolls!" But Floyd simply strives to create works of art that have universal appeal and timeless beauty. "What a privilege to work with a medium I love – wood. The touch, the feel and the smell of wood is a sensual delight in itself. To sculpt in wood is so calming and relaxing, it can be compared only to a sedative," says Floyd. "I am humbled by all the attention given to me for an endeavor which gives me so much pleasure."

Floyd's early dolls sat around the house without any clothes until his wife met Doris Parker at a local market and told her about his dolls. Doris, an expert seamstress, said, "Tell Floyd to bring those naked babies over to my house and I will make clothes for them." She didn't charge any money for her marvelous creations. She traded her work for dolls and now has more of Floyd's dolls than anyone. All are exquisitely dressed in attire appropriate to their era, due to the extensive research she and Mr. Bell have done to assure authenticity for each historical figure.

Toni Bell, Floyd and Sandra's granddaughter, spend a lot of time with her grandparents and playing with dolls. One day as then seven year-old Toni was helping her grandpa stuff bodies for his dolls, she said, "Grandpa, I want you to make me a pretty doll." Floyd said, "What do you mean, pretty? My dolls are pretty!" She said, "Yeah, I

know, but I mean pretty – like Barbie." She showed him her glamorous Barbies in their stunning outfits. Being a devoted grandpa and always enjoying a new challenge, Floyd got some jelutong wood, a carver's delight, and started a slim, shapely black doll for Toni's Christmas gift. She is made entirely of wood and even her hairdo is carved, like the hair of all the Belle Dolls. Then his grown daughters, Karen and Monique, wanted fashion dolls too. As the requests multiplied, the emerging collection was named Toni's Fashion Dolls. They all needed clothes, of course, so Floyd took Toni to some Barbie shows and allowed her to choose the designers she liked best. Soon Toni was dressing her dolls in snazzy outfits and dazzling evening gowns from past eras to the present made by designers such as Anita Diaz and Charlotte Semple. To make the dolls available to more people, Floyd offers cast-resin versions that sell for much less than the wooden dolls. He even developed a line of Toni's Fashion Dolls kits so people could have fun making one themselves.

Floyd has created hundreds of dolls since that first special lady and sells them far and wide. As his appreciation for dolls and their creators grew, he began collecting dolls, pushing aside his concerns about what others might think about a man who buys dolls for himself. "Great dolls, like great art, are just nice to have around you!" he says. "Each doll has its own story to tell. Dolls communicate in a special way. They have a mystical relationship with humans that I call "doll magic." I have watched a hardened construction worker carefully place a rag doll in a safe place on the work site. The doll lay there until someone took it home."

At a time in life when Floyd could choose to relax on a beach, he remains focused on his love of creating inspirational African American figures. He goes to school every day to instruct his students in woodworking and "in lessons of diligence, responsibility, pride and citizenship." He adds, " I feel like I am fulfilling a responsibility to educate our children. Someone has to take the time to contribute and pass on values." May these words carve a tribute of gratitude to Floyd Bell for contributing with dignity and resolve, like the historical figures he has immortalized in wood.

~

Floyd Bell lives in Los Angeles, California, with his wife Sandra and an extended family of dolls. During her weekend visits, his granddaughter Toni gets the opportunity to learn dollmaking.

I met Floyd at a cloth doll convention in San Francisco where he was a keynote speaker and told stories about his students' dollmaking adventures. Material for this profile was taken from Floyd Bell Scholarship Fundraiser booklets, news articles and conversations with Floyd.

Photos: Floyd and his African Grandmother.
Floyd's Ella.
Both reprinted with the permission of Floyd Bell.

Antoinette Bell

Toni's Paragraphs

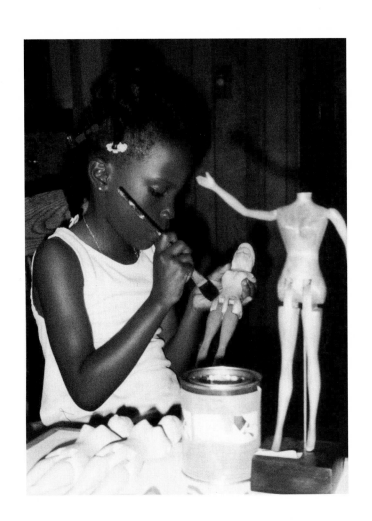

Toni's Paragraphs

I Love Doll Shows

I love to go to doll shows because I see different dolls. Some are big and funny or silly. They all have special things to show and I like that because it makes me feel many ways. If a doll is a play doll, I will play with it a long time because I can do its hair and make bracelets for it. But when I'm at a doll show, I can see clothes for the dolls. I can see shoes for the doll or hair styles to try on my dolls. But what I like best is what kind of pose they do or what their faces express. Maybe their arms will tell you something. I've always liked to play with dolls.

Making Toni's Fashion Dolls With My Grandpa

Making dolls with my grandpa is a lot of work. First you have to buy the wood, then you have to carve it into a doll. Then you have to put it together. What is most important, you have to sand the doll with sandpaper to make it soft and smooth. Next you paint a face on the doll. The wooden dolls have carved hair. I help my grandpa paint the dolls with varnish. This makes them very shiny.

After the dolls are painted and finished, I choose doll clothes for them. Anita Diaz is my fashion designer. She sews beautiful doll clothes. My grandpa and I go to the doll show to pick out doll clothes. I like wide, colorful dresses and skirts. They make the dolls look wonderful.

Hairstyles for Dolls

Dolls with hair are special to me because I can do their hair and that's fun. When I don't have anything to do, I can just go to my room, pick any doll I want and comb its hair for hours. Then I put it down and make a bracelet for it. As you see in this and other paragraphs, I love doing a doll's hair. Sometimes when I see dolls in their boxes, I say, " I hate their hairdo." But other times when a doll is in a box, I say, "What a beautiful hairdo to try to do at home." Sometimes it works, sometimes it doesn't.

Doll Magic

Doll magic is a doll that has what other dolls don't have. Maybe a doll with magic can talk or walk without you holding it or maybe it can eat by itself. Maybe it can sing along with you. Maybe it can skate but the magic doll I like is the doll that sings because it can entertain you. I also like a doll that can walk because it can walk with you and it can make you feel that you're with a friend that isn't even a person.

~

Toni Bell was nine years old when she wrote her paragraphs. She is interested in school, dolls, music and collecting Beanie Babies. She likes to watch the Disney Channel and Nickelodeon. Toni is now ten and in the fifth grade at Saint Eugene's School in Los Angeles.

I met Toni at the home of her grandparents, Floyd and Sandra Bell, where Floyd, Toni and I spent an afternoon doing timed writing together on the family patio.

Photos: Toni varnishing a Toni's Fashion Doll.
A completed Toni's Fashion Doll. Both courtesy of Floyd Bell.

Cara de la Torre

Maryanna Lanier

Never Forgotten

Never Forgotten

Her name was Virginia McClintock. She lived in Missouri in the 1850's. She was the only girl in her family. One day when she was at school a sudden storm came quickly over the prairie and the school. This was not an unusual event in the Midwest. Many a prairie fire had threatened the early settlers as lightning started the prairie grasses to burn and wind made the fires move fast while growing bigger. These 'thunderstorms' still happen. But the storm that day did not start a prairie fire. Lightning struck the school's metal fire escape which was attached to the side of the two-story brick schoolhouse and placed in a position for students on the second floor to be able to escape through the big window that opened onto the top of the fire escape. The children saw a huge, round red ball of brightness, brighter than anything they had ever seen, appear to roll down the fire escape. Then a streak of something bright leaped into the room to something on the hinged part of a desk – Virginia's desk. Virginia was killed by this lightning bolt. No one else was killed or injured that day. The thunder and lightning and rain continued for awhile, then moved out over the prairie and disappeared, as all storms do. The teacher of Virginia's class sent one of the older boys to run to town to tell what had happened.

Virginia's mother was brokenhearted. She grieved and in her grief she worried that someday Virginia would be forgotten because when her mother and fathers' lives were over, there would be no one to remember Virginia, who lived eight years and was dearly loved.

Virginia had a little doll dressed in a blue gingham dress tied with a sash of taffeta. Virginia loved her little doll and played with her every day. The doll was made of porcelain. In those days most children had only one or two toys and if a toy was lost or a doll broken, it probably could not be replaced. Of course Virginia's doll could never have been replaced because it was Virginia's and Virginia loved her. An idea came to Mrs. McClintock. She wrapped the doll in a little quilt that she had made and decided that she would give it to her granddaughter when and if she ever had a granddaughter. And she would tell that granddaughter about Virginia and that she should keep and cherish that doll and when she grew up she should give the doll to her daughter. And that daughter should keep and cherish the doll and give it to her daughter and if every mother in the family as the generations passed did that, Virginia would never be forgotten.

My great-grandmother who is ninety-eight years old, got Virginia's doll from her father's sister who lived on a two hundred acre wheat farm near Hannibal, Missouri. Her name was Bess McClintock and she taught second grade in a red brick schoolhouse much like the one Virginia had attended. She received the doll when she married Clarence McClintock because, as her mother-in-law explained, Clarence had no sisters so there was no daughter to have the doll. My great-great aunt gave the doll to my great-grandmother who gave it to my grandmother who gave it to my mother who gave it to me. I will cherish this doll and will always remember the story of Virginia.

~

Cara de la Torre: "I live in Redmond, Washington. I am fifteen years old and am in ninth grade at Redmond Jr. High. My Grandma, who loves me very much, comes over every Monday after school. She helps me with my homework and we play games and watch TV."

Maryanna Lanier grew up in rural Texas. She moved to California with her husband in 1954 and earned her doctorate in Economics eighteen years later. She taught economics at California State University, Fullterton, until retiring in 1988 when she moved to Washington State to enjoy being near her daughter, son and four grandchildren.

I met Cara, her mother Suzanne and her sister Leanna at an arts booth at a festival in Olympia where they were selling Suzanne's beautiful hand-made sweaters.

*The best and most beautiful things
in the world cannot be seen or even touched.
They must be felt with the heart.*

—Helen Keller 1880-1968

About the Author

Carolyn Michael has been my big sister for 50 years. Even when we were young children, she included me in activities with her friends and was kind, not only to me, but to everyone. Carolyn is a champion of children and was a dedicated educator for more than 20 years. Her deep sensitivity shows itself in her love of the beauty of nature and art. She believes art is an embodiment of spirit that lies waiting to be uniquely expressed in each one of us. It is through her gift of listening and questioning with open-hearted attentiveness that she has midwived the stories in *Enchanted Companions,* written so beautifully by each of her friends.

Virginia Wise
Olympia, Washington

Acknowledgments

My love and gratitude to all who contributed to the creation of this book, including:
Everyone who shared their stories, including those not appearing here.
My parents, Ferd and Audrey Herres, for dolls and everything else.
My son, Ryan Burns, for his strength, music and love; his partner, Tina Routt, for her creativity.
My sister, Virginia Wise, who is always there listening, encouraging, wisely advising.
Janet Yoder, for generous assistance, advice and encouragement every step along the way.
Robby Rudine, for the countless project meetings and his keen and sensitive insights.
Kari Berger, photographer extraordinaire, for the generosity of herself and her time.
Andrea Lewis, for her editorial expertise and getting commas in the right places.
Clare Conrad, for patient listening, seeing the vision and artfully giving the book its final form.

In remembrance of loved ones who helped shape this project:
My son, Brad Burns, whose love, sense of humor and unshakeable belief in me spurred me on.
Mike McManus, who encouraged me to live with passion and purpose and showed the way.
Some Kokita, whose story and graciousness touched me deeply.

For their support, advice and patient encouragement: Marcia Diffendorfer, Jennifer Carrasco, Ward Serrill, Sister Mary Ann Herres, Ann Teplick, Vi Hilbert, Lois Schluter, Heather Reedy, Dan Smith, Pamela Frierson, Carol Severance, Mary Pat Poole, Susan Duncan, Susan Berlin, Floyd Bell, Sharon Winslow, Carly McManus, Glynda Pearce, Kim Ivy, Brad Thompson, Sharon Hagar, Diana Robbins, Jeanette Weston, Jack Le Noir and Maura Shapley at Day Moon Press, Margaret O'Donnell, Ted Cummings, Margaret McGrath, Mark Jaroslav, Naomi Weissman, Diane Fleming, Shaz Davison, Ken Foster, Kim Fleming, Ataa Adjiri, Nicole Brauch, Melissa Kokita, Rosie Kokita, Duse McLean, Barb McConkey, Magrit Baurecht, Erica Sotak, Scot Whitney, Lorenzo and Patricia Leonard, Sheila Habura, Signe Feeney, Debra Van Tuinen, Peg Henry and Lynne Stockwell.

A special thanks to writers who have inspired me: Isabel Allende, Mona Brookes, Maya Angelou, John Irving, J. Ruth Gendler, Tom Robbins and Natalie Goldberg.

Virginia Wise feeding her sister's doll.

Have a doll story you'd like to share?

Submit your typewritten story for a possible future publication. No stories will be returned unless requested and accompanied by a self-addressed stamped envelope.

To order
Enchanted Companions

Send a check or money order for $29.95 in U.S. funds ($39.95 Canadian) to

Storyweaver
1910 East 4th Ave., PMB #91
Olympia, WA 98506–4632

(360) 236-9377 (For VISA/MasterCard)
e-mail: storyweaver4@earthlink.net

Add $5.00 for shipping.
Washington state residents, add 8.25% sales tax.